P9-DMU-155

A Call to Witness

*Reflections on
the Gospel of St. Matthew*

Oliver J. McTernan

THE LITURGICAL PRESS
Collegeville, Minnesota 56321

*I would like to offer a special note of thanks to Sarah
Thomas, May O'Riordan, and Evelyn Zauperman, without
whose encouragement and practical help this book would
not have been written.*

O. J. McTernan

Cover by Robert F. McGovern.

First published in Great Britain by Fount Paperbacks, London, in 1988.

Copyright © Oliver McTernan 1988. All rights reserved. This edition for the United
States of America published by The Liturgical Press, Collegeville, Minnesota.

1   2   3   4   5   6   7   8

Library of Congress Cataloging-in-Publication Data

McTernan, Oliver J.
    A call to witness : reflections on the Gospel of St. Matthew /
Oliver J. McTernan.
        p. cm.
    Includes bibliographical references.
    ISBN 0-8146-1838-3
    1. Bible. N.T. Matthew—Commentaries.   I. Title.
BS2575.3.M37   1989   89-38222
226.2'07—dc20   CIP

Contents

CHAPTER 1

An Unexpected Pregnancy

. . . Her husband Joseph, being a man of honor and wanting to spare her publicity, decided to divorce her informally. . . .

—Matt 1:18-25

It may come as a surprise to anyone unfamiliar with the Gospel that Matthew's story of Jesus begins with the trauma of an unexpected pregnancy. We know only too well how such a pregnancy can cause considerable embarrassment and anxiety, especially to the woman, even in today's more liberal and permissive society. In those days the anxiety would have been even more acute. Had Joseph mishandled the situation, it would have meant exposure to public ridicule and perhaps even death for Mary. According to the custom of the time, betrothal meant that, even though they were not yet married, they were emotionally bound, and already equally committed to each other. The religious law required death by stoning as the price to be paid for such an infidelity as adultery.

Matthew's story draws our attention mainly to the reaction of Joseph, who must have been deeply disturbed and confused at the very thought of Mary's betrayal of his love and trust. Joseph's initial reaction was quite predictable: as a man of honor he decided to divorce Mary, to send her away. Yet his anger was clearly tempered by his love and feelings for her, and he wanted to protect her from further hurt. By divorcing her privately he hoped and believed that he could save her the pain of public exposure. This suggests that Joseph was totally confused by the

5

whole affair. Either he had not really thought how Mary would cope as a single parent, let alone avoid inevitable exposure as an unmarried mother; or else if he had, he was the sort of person who was not prepared to compromise the norms and values which he had learned from his religious upbringing. Either way, the pain which comes from misunderstanding and loss of human trust must have been truly severe for both of them.

This episode in the life of Joseph and Mary has been interpreted in a number of ways. My own impression is that Joseph may well have found himself caught in that familiar human predicament where a person is torn between feelings and principles. His principles apparently would not allow him to live under the pretense that would be necessary if he were to marry Mary. He knew that the child was not his, and he felt obliged to act in accordance with the law. He could see no alternative but to send her away.

But besides being a man of honor, Joseph was also a man of faith. His traditional Jewish faith required of him an openness of mind and a willingness to accept God's intervention in the affairs of human life. These he demonstrated in his reaction to God's indirect intervention in this time of personal crisis— Matthew tells us that he learned in a dream of the role God had played in the matter. Joseph's response to this God-given guidance was to set aside his fears and doubts and to take another look at the painful event which threatened to separate Mary and himself. Through his faith he was able to discover a new depth of understanding and to turn this most painful and traumatic episode into a moment of real grace, a time for real human growth.

What Matthew offers us in this opening chapter of his Gospel is a very human story, which carries within it a profound insight into the nature of the Christian faith. It is hardly by accident that he chooses to relate it right at the beginning of his account of the life, death, and resurrection of Jesus Christ. The story, for me at least, sets the tone for what is to follow. It is as though Matthew were warning us to be under no illusion about the Gospel. It is a message for real life, leaving no room for make-believe or pretense. The God of this Gospel, the God of Jesus, is for real people.

This means that in our own search for faith we must not be tempted to look for some sort of shield or protection against life's problems. The faith which Matthew presents is not a passport or exit visa through which to escape from some of the harsher realities that life brings our way. On the contrary, the Christian faith, properly lived, can even put us in the way of such problems.

This was certainly Mary's experience. Her quiet and more or less predictable routine was suddenly thrown into confusion simply because of her willingness to allow God the freedom to direct her life. It was her faith, her openness to God, which created the situation that caused her to suffer such doubt and uncertainty. But it was also her faith that enabled her to discover, through this painful process, the only way to true spiritual growth and fulfillment. Mary's witness, her trust, and above all, her readiness to serve God's purpose without counting the personal cost bring us directly to the heart of the Christian belief.

To anyone already committed to the Christian faith who rereads it, this story should come as a sober reminder that God is frequently to be found in events which appear to be outside the accepted norms of the day. The God of Matthew's Gospel, in other words, is not averse to roaming beyond the pale. This thought can be deeply disturbing for those who have been brought up to look for God solely within the walls of their local church or in the observance of certain religious codes and practices.

The circumstances surrounding the birth of Jesus were clearly far from what people imagined the coming of the Christ would be like. It is as if God chose to slip through the back door of human history unnoticed. He arrived at a time when he was least expected and in the least acceptable manner. It cannot come as too much of a surprise to us, then, to find that Matthew's claim that Jesus was the Christ gave great offense to those religious leaders who prided themselves on their self-proclaimed knowledge of the ways of God. And in fact, who could blame them for failing to understand the significance of the birth of a child to such a lowly couple from a place as obscure and unimportant as Nazareth? Their initial lack of vigilance could be reasonably excused, and yet their own religious traditions should have prepared them for such an unexpected intervention of God. In the past, on many occasions, their God had shown himself to be far from predictable. This was most noticeable in the sort of people he chose to be his prophets.

Matthew's story reminds us that it is the same unpredictable God who reaches out in search of us today. The vision of faith which it offers cannot be limited to religious practices alone, for faith should inspire us to discover the fullness of our human life. It should teach us to embrace every human experience—life's painful moments as well as its joyful ones. Faith should enable us to find what is beautiful, truthful, and just in every human experience. Above all, faith should teach us to trust in the power of God to achieve his purpose for creation. Faith understood in this way can never allow us to abdicate our responsibilities toward life itself.

Marx could not have described religion as the opium of the people if so many Christians in his day had not been so ready to separate their beliefs from life. Throughout history, religion has been misused to justify indifference or inactivity, especially in the face of human misery and suffering. Religion has so often been seen as the great ally of the *status quo,* allowing unjust situations to go on unchallenged and unchanged. The Second Vatican Council clearly recognized the risk involved when faith is separated from ordinary day-to-day life; it saw it as tantamount to sowing the seeds of atheism. In the document in which it deals with the role of the Church in the world today, the Council claims that "to the extent that believers are careless about their faith, or present its teachings falsely, or even fail in their religious, moral, or social life, they must be said to conceal, rather than to reveal, the true nature of God and religion" (par. 19).

The idea of a God intimately involved in human affairs is, for most people, quite challenging, if not frightening. So much so that it often appears to me that no sooner had God involved himself in our human history than believers were searching for ways of disengaging him. A God who confined himself to the purely spiritual would somehow be manageable and therefore more acceptable. And we would avoid the risk of God getting in the way as we pursue our secular goals—while at the same time have a mental refuge available for those times when the going gets rough. Our problem is, of course, that God will not allow us to confine him in this way. Through the birth of Jesus, God intimately involved himself in our human affairs, and the good news Matthew brings is that he is here to stay.

Once faith opens us up to discover the presence of God in our lives, we frequently find that the access which God requires goes far beyond what we were initially willing to give. God, as both Mary and Joseph discovered, frequently demands that we set aside our immediate plans and that we learn, sometimes painfully, to let go of the tight personal control most of us claim over our daily lives. In coming to know God we have to learn to find a new sense of security, based solely upon our personal trust in the power of God's love.

The God whom this story from Matthew's Gospel brings into our lives can at times behave like the unwanted caller, who always seems to pick the most inconvenient moments to intrude. Or else like the awkward guest, who hangs around our home making what often appear to be most unreasonable demands on our limited time and resources. The price we must be prepared to pay for the faith which Matthew's Gospel asks of us is a readiness to set aside even our legitimate personal interests. Only then will God find sufficient space to enter into our lives in a fully meaningful way.

The story of Mary and Joseph's trauma makes one thing quite clear: that Christian faith involves more than our intellectual assent to a number of dogmas. It is an all-embracing encounter with life in its fullness, an encounter with God which involves the heart as well as the mind, the will as well as the intellect.

CHAPTER 2

A Group of Extraordinary Visitors

They went into the house and when they saw the child with his mother, Mary, they knelt down and worshipped him.
—Matt 2:1-12

When we pick up a modern translation of the Gospels and find that the language is familiar, we easily forget that this is literature of a form quite different from that which we would normally read today. We are tempted to look upon the Gospels simply as stories, as literal accounts of what actually happened in the life of Jesus. But to approach them in this way is to forget that their authors' prime purpose was to communicate their belief in Jesus as the Christ, that is, as the one whom God had promised to send.

Matthew, in order to do this effectively, made full use of the various literary forms which were widely understood and accepted in his day. The problem this presents for us is that it is not always possible to distinguish between them, especially when it comes to distinguishing legend from historical fact.

This is particularly true of the story of the Magi. We do not know how much of Matthew's account of this extraordinary visit is rooted in fact or how much in legend. A quick glance at the text, however, clearly shows that the popular image of the Magi as three oriental-type kings comes more from a later tradition than it does from the brief details Matthew himself provided. He does not seem to be too concerned about establishing the full identity of these wise men. He gives them no names, nor does he tell us how many of them arrived at the house of Mary and Joseph.

To understand why such details seem to be unimportant to him, we must remember that it was not Matthew's intention to write a simple biographical account of Jesus' early life. He was more concerned to make a statement about faith. And he included the story of these strange visitors, be it based on fact or on legend, simply to throw more light on the real nature of the Christian faith.

If we examine the Magi story in its immediate context, we see how Matthew presents the birth of Jesus as an event so normal and insignificant that it could easily have passed unnoticed, had it not been for the arrival of this inquisitive group of strangers. It was their presence which provoked a reaction from the authorities. It was, of course, a negative reaction, but given the fact that Palestine was then under Roman occupation and that the civil and religious leaders were caught up in the sort of compromises and political intrigues which are inevitable in such circumstances, it is not surprising that they should have greatly feared what the Magi had to say. The birth of someone claiming to be their king would have caused them considerable anxiety: it could so easily destabilize the delicate balance of power which had come to exist between themselves and their Roman overlords. It would have seemed perfectly reasonable to them, therefore, that any such claim should be promptly refuted and the claimant removed as quickly as possible from the political scene.

The point Matthew was seeking to communicate to his immediate listeners through this story should, of course, have been quite obvious to them. The religious leaders, who should have been ready to accept Jesus as God's Promised One, were in fact the first to reject him, while those least prepared to receive him were the first to seek him out and acknowledge his presence. This must have sounded quite scandalous to Matthew's listeners. He was telling them, in effect, that people whom they considered to be unacceptable in the sight of God were actually among the first to encounter God incarnate.

But what does this story tell us about faith and our own relationship with God? For me, Matthew is once more underlining a very important truth, namely that God reaches out to us in the ordinary events of our lives. This is what we mean when we say that we believe in an incarnate God. There are no barriers, no goals to achieve; God has made himself totally available to us in the life we are living.

Yet our response to this wonderful gesture can be similar to that of those religious leaders who were too quick to reject Jesus as the Christ. We can only too easily be so preoccupied with our own plans and concerns that we fail to see and understand the true significance of what happens in our ordinary day-to-day lives. Everyday events in which God is truly present can pass us by unnoticed, simply because we were expecting to find our God elsewhere.

Forgetting that God has chosen to dwell in the midst of human life, we continually follow our natural tendency to search for him in its more spectacular and extraordinary events. The thought of God being caught up in the phenomenon of an apparently moving statue is, for some at least, far more attractive than the thought of his being present in our moments of loneliness. It would seem that we find it easier to believe in a God who surrounds himself with power, mystique, and majesty than in a God who is content to seek rest in the arms of a young mother.

The God before whom Matthew's wise men knelt and worshiped can become so uncomfortably close to us that we take fright and retreat behind barriers of our own making. Frightened by what God may ask of us, we are often unable or unwilling to surrender in the spirit of obedient love displayed by the Magi. We forget that the only treasure which God expects of us, and which we can truly give, is an openness of mind and heart. As the prophet Joel proclaimed, a true relationship with God demands that we "rend our hearts and not our garments" (Joel 2:12-30). Mere outward observance, then, is not sufficient to sustain that new level of relationship with our God, who has chosen to dwell among us.

But Matthew had another message which he wanted to get across to his listeners. By introducing the visit of the Magi, he was able to proclaim his belief in the universality of God's love. The brief description he gives of this first encounter between Jesus and the gentile world conveys to us the image of how Jew and Gentile, as well as the highly esteemed and the lowly, can, in the presence of Christ, find their true identity as God's children. St. Paul was more explicit when he wrote in his Letter to the Galatians (3:28) that "there is no such thing as Jew and Greek, slave and freeman; for you are all one person in Christ Jesus." God's love embraces all races, so no single group or tribe can claim it as its exclusive right.

The concept no doubt shocked those of his listeners who found themselves caught up in the struggle to protect their own national and spiritual identity from foreign influence. Matthew is clearly repudiating, as foreign to the mind of God, any racism or extreme nationalism which, of its very nature, excludes the rightful claims of others. The true dignity of each person comes not from membership of any particular tribe or nation but from his or her unique relationship with God, who is the source of all human life. Once we accept this belief in the universality of God's love, it will have profound implications for the way we live, and especially for the way we relate to others.

The most immediate and most obvious consequence of such a belief is that we should be willing to protest against any form of discrimination against people on the grounds of race, color, condition in life, or religion. But our public protest will be credible only if it goes hand in hand with a sincere effort to root out from our lives all traces of these same forms of prejudice. The problem is, of course, that frequently we are not even aware of our own prejudices, some of which we may have grown to accept over the years as "normal" attitudes. Coming to grips with them can be a most painful experience, which many would prefer to avoid. Yet if we fail to do so, we shall undoubtedly be prevented from growing in the way that God intends.

Sadly, the Church itself has not always lived up to the gospel expectations in this respect. There are many episodes in our history where Christians, misguidedly, have been in the forefront of promoting active policies of discrimination. I find it particularly painful when I recall the role several generations of Christians have played in spreading anti-Semitism. All the same, the guilt we can feel as we openly recognize such mistakes should not inhibit us from being in the forefront of the struggle against racism and discrimination of any kind today.

If we believe in the universality of God's love, we must also accept that there is "an inescapable duty" to make ourselves the neighbor of every person, no matter who that person is *(The Church in the Modern World,* par. 27; Documents of Vatican II). And we must also recognize that we cannot "truly pray to God the Father of All, if we treat any people in other than brotherly fashion" *(Vatican II, Non-Christian Religion,* par. 5). But there is also another dimension to the belief that all peoples are called to share in God's love. By learning to respect and share our differences, we soon discover that, far from being threatened, we are in fact enriched. I, personally, have experienced this since I came to work in the parish of Notting Hill, where we have so many races and cultures living side by side.

In our parish program we have encouraged the celebration of differences by inviting our various ethnic groups to host social evenings, during which they can share something of their cultural heritages, including their music and food, with the wider community. This has been a most enriching experience for those who have opened themselves to it. Of course, it required them to let go of some of their old ways of thinking, but I firmly believe that it is only when we learn to share in this way—that is, when we learn to be open to being enriched by those who are different—that we begin to discover a real sense of our own incompleteness, and hence, of our need for God and for others. It is through this sort of involvement in the cultural life of others that we discover a fuller meaning in the belief that God did not create the human person to be a solitary being.

We know, from what the Bible has to say about creation, that we were made to live in communion with others. We know from human experience how failure to enter into relationships with others can prevent us from fully developing our human gifts. But what applies on this individual level of our human experience is equally valid when it comes to intergroup or intertribal experience. I believe that it is only in communion with those of different cultures and different ethnic backgrounds that we can discover the true value of our own cultural and ethnic identity. It is also through this communion with one another that we can begin to discover, and to reflect on, something of the true nature and richness of God himself. Racial discrimination, in any of its forms, presents a real barrier to spiritual and human growth.

CHAPTER 3

A Moment of Truth

Then Jesus was led by the Spirit out into the Wilderness to be tempted by the devil. He fasted for forty days and forty nights, after which he was very hungry.
—Matt 4:1-11

By the time Matthew's Gospel came to be written, Jesus' followers firmly believed that he was in fact the Christ, the Chosen One of God, who had come to fulfill the promises God had made to their ancestors. Their genuine desire to share this belief with the wider Jewish community undoubtedly influenced the way in which they presented the Gospel message. Throughout the Gospel they frequently drew parallels between the actions of Jesus and the great events and figures of their own history.

This approach is very obvious in Matthew's story of Jesus' temptation in the wilderness. Any devout Jew listening to it would have been reminded immediately of Moses: he too spent forty days and nights fasting in the wilderness before proclaiming God's Law to the people (Exod 34:28). Again, the devout Jew would have recalled that just as Matthew told how Jesus' loyalty was tested during his time in the desert, so the Book of Deuteronomy recorded how God had tested the loyalty of his people, Israel, as they wandered for forty years in the wilderness (Deut 8:2-8).

How much of the temptation story is rooted in fact and how much in legend, we simply do not know. But these questions are not so important if we remember that Matthew's prime purpose in telling the story of Jesus in the wilderness was to help his listeners understand the kind of Christ or Messiah that God

16

was calling Jesus to be. His role was to be quite different from what most of Matthew's audience had been taught to expect. They had been looking forward to the day when, as a nation, they would be freed from the Roman occupation and would openly enjoy the privileges and glory which they felt belonged to them as God's people. This, they believed, was the way in which God meant to vindicate, before all the other nations, their faith and trust in him. The very possibility of a Messiah who refused to play the role of liberator in this sense must have come as a bitter disappointment. Matthew was warning them that Jesus had no intention of working miracles just to win their favor. This was not God's way of relating to those whom he loved.

Matthew's use of the word "temptation" did not, of course, carry the negative overtones it does today. To be tempted meant to be tested more in a positive than in a negative sense. The time Jesus spent in the wilderness gave him the opportunity to discover his true God-given identity. And Matthew's account of it gives us the opportunity to reflect on the nature of our own relationship with God.

I never appreciated the effect a trip to the desert could have on a person's faith until I had the chance to spend a few days in the Sinai. This experience gave me a much clearer understanding of why the wilderness has always been seen as a real testing ground for belief. I set out with eight others on an organized tour to Mount Sinai, the site where, according to tradition, Moses received the Ten Commandments. We were a diverse group, brought together solely by our curiosity to see what life in the desert was really like. The hostile nature of our surroundings was brought home to us when the driver of the Land Rover, which was carrying all our food and clothing, got lost. By the time he caught up with us several hours later, we were all feeling extremely vulnerable.

Later, during the night, I decided to wander a few hundred yards away from our camp by myself. The experience of sitting there alone in such a dark and hostile environment greatly increased my own sense of vulnerability. I realized how much I had come to depend upon the support of my fellow travelers, even though all of them were strangers to me. And more important, I became deeply aware of my own need to believe in a personal God who loved me. This brief exposure to desert life was suffi- cient for me to understand how important a sense of being vul- nerable is in helping us to grow and mature in faith. When all the familiar props have been removed, we soon recognize our human incompleteness—and that is something we have to ac- knowledge before we can even begin to give God his rightful place in our lives. It is, therefore, not surprising that generations of believers should have found the desert experience essential to growth in faith or that Jesus himself, while preparing for his public mission, used the desert to affirm his own belief and to demon- strate his love for God the Father.

The Bible has little to tell us about the devil, other than that he is the one who gets in the way—who seeks to upset God's plans. And in Matthew's story of Jesus in the wilderness, the devil plays this traditional role. However, Jesus does not allow the ap- parent reasonableness of the devil's arguments to distract him from his vocation, which is to serve God with all his heart, with all his soul, with all his strength (cf. Deut 6:5). He would not compromise his faith by putting God to the test as his ancestors had done at Massah in the desert (Exod 17:1-7). Matthew's mes- sage is clear: Jesus is the Son of God; his desert experience proved that the Word of God was written on his heart (Deut 6:6). Satan could not get in his way.

The Gospel sets the scene for the first temptation by stating that Jesus was hungry. The devil tries to exploit the situation by playing on this weakness. Jesus is in need of food, so it would be perfectly reasonable for him to obtain it by using his God- given powers and turning "stones into loaves" (Matt 4:3). What could be wrong with that? Surely he should take advantage of his privileged position in his own hour of need. But Jesus refused to become a wonder worker for his own sake. His sole purpose in life was to serve God. He did not want attention for himself. So hunger gave him no excuse to misuse, even in private, the gifts that God had entrusted to him. Jesus realized that his loyalty was being tested. He stood firm, despite his weak condition. Later in life, his loyalty was to be tested in a similar manner when, as he hung on the cross, the passers-by tempted him to use his powers to save himself (Matt 27:10). His experience in the wilderness must have strengthened him for that moment.

The devil, having failed to exploit his physical weakness, turned immediately to Jesus' spiritual strength—his love of God. If Jesus were to throw himself from the parapet of the Temple (4:5), God would have an opportunity to demonstrate his presence as someone who cares. The argument, of course, was perverse. What the devil wanted was to get Jesus to seek assurance by forcing God to show himself as a protector of those he loves. Jesus refused to put God to the test; real faith does not call for such guarantees.

Lastly, the devil offered to help Jesus fulfill his mission. There was no need, he suggested, to waste time. Jesus could, if he wanted, take immediate control of "all the kingdoms of the world and their splendor" (4:9)—but at a price which made the proposed shortcut totally unacceptable. Jesus refused to be enslaved by the desire for worldly power, and the devil, who had by now revealed himself as the one who hinders the way of God, was finally dismissed: "Be off, Satan." Peter, later in the Gospel, received a similar rebuke when he tried to prevent Jesus from following a course of action which would eventually lead him to the cross (Matt 16:23).

The story of Jesus in the wilderness should be a great help to us in our own search for faith. Besides providing a valuable insight into the way God wants to relate to us, it identifies some of the obstacles that can so easily get in the way of that relationship. The apparent reasonableness with which the devil argues alerts us to the need for a regular and honest examination, in the light of faith, of all our actions and attitudes. Without such scrutiny we can so easily—if unintentionally—drift into a way of thinking and living which eventually would alienate us from God. Matthew challenges us first of all to clarify our own image and understanding of God. This is an essential starting point in the search for a mature faith.

A girl in her late teens once came to me in a confused state. Despite her very privileged upbringing, her life had become so boring that, in her search for excitement, she had drifted into circles where heavy drinking and casual sex were the norm. She soon found not only that her new lifestyle was a source of further confusion but that it was alienating her from her own family, whom she still loved. She wanted me to help. We met for a few times to talk about her problems, but what I had to say seemed to make little difference to her behavior. One day she came to me in an angry mood. "You religious people are all the same. You are full of smooth talk about how much God loves everyone, especially those in need. What help has God offered me? Why has God not intervened in my life to stop me from doing such harm to myself?" Her outburst uncovered an understanding of God which had not matured much since her childhood. She was still living with an image of God as the old white bearded man in the sky who pulls all the strings. And since this God was apparently ignoring her particular cry for help, her anger was quite understandable.

Her story is all too familiar. The image of God which frequently presents a stumbling block to those who are in search of faith, or in real need of God's help, is not always the image we find reflected in the words of the Gospel. The popular—distorted—image of God as a benevolent grandfather figure can easily get in the way of genuine faith.

The God to whom Matthew introduces us does not offer bribes in the hope that we will come to believe in him, nor does he perform any spectacular feats to impress. The faith which we find expressed in the life of Jesus is essentially a partnership founded on love that is freely given. God does not force himself upon us. His love for us is neither overprotective nor possessive. He even allows us enough personal space to make the mistake of rejecting his love. We are not created with an in-built program which restricts us in this respect. The God of the Judeo-

Christian faith has no need of a love that does not spring from the human heart. The love he wants leaves open the possibility of our being able to say no to his advances.

A faith which grows out of this understanding of God will not depend on miracles, nor will it attempt to bring God under our own control. It can even tolerate God's apparent silence or inactivity when we are feeling vulnerable or most in need. In other words, it can give us the courage to embrace all life's experiences and to avoid the temptation to circumvent things we find unattractive or painful. Matthew's faith will not allow us to live in a world of make-believe or pretense. It prevents us from re-creating the image of God according to our own wishes and needs. A god who allowed himself to be treated like a genie in a lamp, intervening continually for our convenience in order to secure our love, would be as contemptible as a god who forced us to cooperate with some predetermined plan. God seeks our cooperation, our love, and he never forces them from us.

Few people are able to make a journey into the desert. But most of us experience our human vulnerability many times during the course of our lives. When confronted with our vulnerability, we not uncommonly seek refuge immediately, either in material goods or social status, or else in alcohol or some other drug. Matthew offers a real alternative. Jesus' experience showed how genuine faith can turn these threatening moments into a time for real spiritual growth. Temptation is not to be feared as something totally negative—a time when we experience only failure. On the contrary, we must learn to embrace our own experiences of weakness and vulnerability as opportunities to affirm our faith and our trust in God. It is in this sense that St. James could write to a community of recently converted Christians: "You will always have your trials, but, when they come, try to treat them as a happy privilege; you understand that your faith is only put to the test to make you patient, but patience too is to have its practical results, so that you will become fully developed, complete, with nothing missing" (Jas 1:2-4). A mature faith should help us to develop, not diminish, our human potential.

CHAPTER 4

A New Vision

Seeing the crowds, he went up the hill. Then he sat down and was joined by his disciples. Then he began to speak. This is what he taught them:
   "How happy are the poor in spirit. . . ."
                                           —Matt 5:1-12

When Jesus sat down to teach, no one kept a written record of his words. His message was learned by heart and passed on by word of mouth. Some of his sayings were eventually written down, and Matthew undoubtedly made use of this material when compiling his own Gospel. His purpose in writing it, however, was not to provide an accurate historical account of the life of Jesus for posterity. Matthew was rather writing for his own community of Christian converts. He was anxious to help them to understand the full implications of their faith in Jesus as the Messiah—and, of course, to communicate this belief to others, especially their Jewish neighbors. This ambition influenced the technique and style which Matthew used to compile and present the traditions that had been accumulated concerning the life and teaching of Jesus. The Sermon on the Mount (Matt 5–7) is a good example of this. Matthew has evidently brought together various sayings of Jesus and presented them in the literary form of a single sermon. The significance of this technique may not be immediately obvious to us, but it would not have been overlooked by the people for whom he was writing. The mountain location for the sermon would have given them the clue to Matthew's plan. In the Hebrew tradition mountains were closely associated with the revelation of God. Moses had received the Law on a mountain (see Exod 19:20). Matthew wanted to present Jesus as the new Moses, which would give him the authority to teach a new law. He also believed that the spirit of this new law was to be found in those sayings of Jesus which he had gathered into a single discourse.

The sermon begins with a reminder that the messianic age has come. The prophets had always taught that God would eventually intervene on behalf of the poor. Jesus' opening proclamation suggests that this was indeed happening. His words, "happy the poor in spirit" (v. 3), clearly endorse the message of the prophet Isaiah:

> The spirit of the Lord has been given to me, for the Lord has anointed me. He has sent me to bring good news to the poor . . . (Isa 61:1).

Matthew affirms Jesus' true identity as the Messiah, the Anointed One of God, and places his teaching firmly within the tradition of the prophets. Jesus had come to fulfill both the Law and the prophets.

The direct link between the words of Jesus and the teaching of the prophets is important. It should help us avoid the temptation to spiritualize his message to the point where we lose sight of its original meaning. In the course of history diverse attempts have been made to explain the words "poor in spirit." Some have gone so far as to argue that Jesus actually meant those who have wealth but are emotionally detached from it. A spirit of interior detachment is, of course, important, but to claim that what Jesus is teaching can be reduced merely to an attitude of mind would be to deprive his message of its full richness.

When he spoke of the poor, Jesus, like the prophets before him, was referring to the destitute, the landless, and the outcasts, all of whom were completely powerless with no one to defend their rights or to champion their cause. Lacking all influence and prestige, they had become the despised of their society. In other words, Jesus' message is directed to those who are so utterly vulnerable that they have no alternative but to place their complete trust in God. The good news he proclaimed was that God had not betrayed their trust. God had not failed them.

Jesus assured the poor that God had not let their cry go unheard; neither had he overlooked the injustice of their situation. The curse of poverty, which had isolated them from society, had failed to separate them from God. Or rather, it was their destitute condition, their total vulnerability, which had brought God closer to them. God's bias was in their favor; God was to be found in the midst of their destitution. *This* is what makes the poor "blessed."

Jesus was offering the poor not a pious hope for future happiness but a message to bring them real joy there and then, despite their pitiful condition. Their happiness was not to depend upon external circumstances. It was to be rooted in awareness of God's bias and of his presence in their midst. And because it could not be taken from them, because it offered them real security despite the insecure circumstances in which they were forced to live, this awareness of God's favor would be a source of continual joy and happiness for the poor.

Jesus was not, of course, claiming that poverty as such is a virtue, a God-given gift to be safeguarded at all costs. His message was that God is predisposed toward those who are vulnerable and that God's closeness, not their poverty, is the real source of joy and happiness in the lives of the poor.

Jesus' words, "happy the poor in spirit," took on a whole new meaning for me after my first visit to Ethiopia. I went expecting to find no sense of joy or happiness in a country where poverty is so widespread and so extreme that the average life expectancy is a mere forty years. But my experience was quite the opposite. Among the tribal peoples of the southern highlands, a region where everyone is poor and where most people are suffering from some form of disease, I discovered real faith-inspired joy.

One particular experience immediately comes to mind. I had been invited to take part in a prayer meeting in an isolated mountain village. The Christians in that area had no church building, so they met regularly for prayer in one another's homes. By the time I arrived the prayer meeting had been in progress for at least two hours. To enter the hut I had to stoop low. It was extremely dark inside—there was no electricity in the area, and they could not afford to buy candles. Gradually, I realized that there must be at least forty people, young and old, sitting there on the floor, completely absorbed in prayer.

At the end of the service everyone present was invited to share in the simple meal of the poor—boiled corn and salted coffee. But before we ate a young girl entered the hut, carrying an old tin can full of water—water for which she would have had to walk at least four miles. This was offered to each of the guests in turn so that they could wash their hands before eating. In a most graceful and reverent way, the young girl moved from guest to guest. It was a genuinely sacred moment, a time when God's presence was truly felt. I was so deeply touched that, brushing aside all the warnings I had received about the risk of hepatitis, I joined in the meal that was set before us. In sharing their corn and coffee, I found myself at one with a people who were destitute in the material sense yet rich in human dignity, disease ridden yet truly joyful in spirit. They firmly believed that God was with them in the midst of their destitution, and it was through this faith that they had learned to cope with the inevitable frustrations that come with poverty and disease.

Yet religion for them was not a cheap substitute for opium. Their embrace was too warm and their pain too real for them to be living in that sort of trance. Among those Ethiopian Christians I was able to experience, in the midst of real want, a faith similar to that reflected in the words of the Jewish prophet Habakkuk, who proclaimed:

> Even though the fig-trees have no fruit and no grapes grow on the vines, even though the olive-crop fails, and the fields produce no corn, even though the sheep all die and the cattle stalls are empty, I will still be joyful and glad, because the Lord God is my Savior (Hab 3:17-18).

That was the quality of faith that Jesus himself endorsed when he proclaimed that the poor are "happy." And that is the faith which enables the Ethiopian Christian to survive, even in the midst of extreme want.

But the poor are not the only ones to enjoy God's bias. The gentle, the mourner, and those who hunger and thirst for what is right can also be "happy" in the knowledge of God's presence. The gentleness or meekness to which Jesus refers is not that of the timid, subservient, or naturally sweet-tempered type of person. It is the gentleness of those who prefer not to go around imposing their rights, who have learned to surrender themselves totally to God and to be patient with him. The mourners are those who know a feeling of emptiness in their lives. The seekers of right are those who possess an insatiable thirst for truth. Each of these qualities can bring a person closer to God, who is inevitably attracted to the vulnerability of the poor, to the patience of the gentle, to the emptiness of the mourner, and to the openness of mind and heart that can be found in the one who seeks truth and justice. It is in their lack of influence and power and in their public loss of esteem that the poor, the hungry, the gentle, and the mourner discover their human incompleteness. All of these experiences have one thing in common: they allow space for God. The very people whom society overlooks have become the models upon which the disciples, the new people of God, should learn to base their own lifestyle.

Those opening words of the Sermon on the Mount reveal just how radical Jesus' message is. They are a forceful reminder that none of those called to follow Jesus, the Anointed One, can at the same time seek security in wealth, high social status, or half-truths. The sense of security which really matters in life will come only when they have learned to recognize their human incompleteness. For only then will they discover their real need for God. And the good news which Jesus brings is that God is to be found in precisely that recognition of human incompleteness.

So a sense of incompleteness is not something to be feared. No one should give in to the temptation to run away from it—

to do so would be to deprive oneself of the source of true happiness. This insight lies at the core of the sermon which Matthew compiled from the sayings of Jesus. It is this message which must now find its way into the human heart (cf. Deut 6:6).

Compassion, purity, and a commitment to peace are to be the characteristics of Jesus' disciples—the hallmark of the new law which he taught them. True happiness can only be found in the pursuit of these virtues. The practice of mercy, or compassion, which had always been seen as a truly God-like quality, must now become the norm by which the disciples learn to relate to those about them. Mercy means more than a willingness to reach out to others: it demands from the disciple a high level of sensitivity, a real desire to enter fully into the world of another person, so much so that he or she can sense that person's pain. In practice, this means a disciple must always be ready to accept intrusions in life and to allow others to impose limitations upon his or her time. Jesus pointed to an outstanding example of this in the story of the good samaritan (Luke 10:29-37).

Purity of heart is not just another way of referring to a chaste body. In Hebrew thought, the heart was at the center of all human activity, the place where decisions were made and where a person's true character was shaped. Jesus wanted his disciples to be singleminded, sincere, and straightforward in their whole approach to life and their actions to be without ambiguity or duplicity. Chastity of the body is only one of the attributes of a pure heart.

The disciple is also called to be a peacemaker. The Book of Genesis introduces us to the Hebrew word for peace, *shalom*, which expresses the idea of completeness, or wholeness. It evokes a situation in which the human person lives in harmony with God, with nature, and with himself. But while it had this cosmic dimension, peace for the Hebrew was firmly rooted in concrete realities of the here and now. The prophets continually challenged the idea that peace could be established where there was no concern for justice. Isaiah, for example, identified the exploitation of the weak and powerless as the greatest obstacle to the realization of *shalom.*

> "Remove the chains of oppression," he warned, "and the yoke of injustice, and let the oppressed go free. Share your food with the hungry and open your homes to the homeless poor. Give clothes to those who have nothing to wear . . ." (Isa 58:7).

In other words, justice is a prerequisite for peace. This means that in their own work for peace the disciples would want to do more than eliminate conflict between their fellow human beings.

By the time the Gospel was written, Matthew's community was no stranger to hostility and rejection. Its members had even been barred from using the synagogue by the religious leaders, who were anxious about the message they taught. Matthew reminds his community that Jesus himself had warned them that such reactions were inevitable. Their new lifestyle would be more of a threat than a comfort to those around them. Their radical search for the security that comes from God and can only be found in vulnerability, patience, and emptiness—as it is by those who are poor, meek, and mournful—would be bound to disturb anyone who sought security in wealth or status. All the same, calumny, abuse, and even persecution cannot deprive the true disciple of the happiness which comes from knowing God's presence.

Although today we are far removed from the immediate concerns of Matthew's community of converts, the force of his message still holds good. The opening verses of the Sermon on the Mount, the Beatitudes, still point the way to the gift of mature faith. They remind us that Christian faith is not a disposition of the mind, that the gospel calls for much more than an internal detachment from material possessions. Knowing God's bias, we come to realize that our lifestyle matters to him, that possessions get in the way of his love. And if we are tempted to doubt the message of the Beatitudes on this point, we would do well to reflect on the story of the rich young man who had faith, but not enough faith to make him a Christian, a follower of the Anointed One (Matt 19:16-30).

On the other hand, there is no virtue in the poverty of an empty room if we remain jealous of our time, our reputation, or our own need for privacy. Poverty which allows us to become totally self-absorbed in the pursuit of other goals, no matter how legitimate these may appear, is delusive and spiritually damaging. The ideal of poverty which Matthew's Gospel puts before us must be understood in the light of Jesus' call for meekness, compassion, purity, and work for justice and peace. The practice of Christian poverty lies essentially in the quest for those attitudes and conditions that allow a person to be totally available to God and neighbor. This should never be considered a mere option; it is a prerequisite for the full pursuit of those other virtues which should characterize the life of every Christian. An awareness of this calls for a continual examination of lifestyle, both at an individual and at a community level.

It is not always easy for us in our affluent Western society to distinguish between our legitimate material needs and those possessions which are truly superfluous. This problem was clearly recognized by the Synod of Bishops which met in Rome in 1971. What the Synod had to say regarding the life of the Church can be applied equally to the individual who is in search of a mature Christian faith:

> In regard to temporal possessions, whatever be their use, it must never happen that the evangelical witness which the Church is required to give, becomes ambiguous. The preservation of certain positions of privilege must constantly be submitted to the test of this principle. Although in general it is difficult to draw a line between what is needed for right use and what is demanded by prophetic witness, we must certainly keep firmly to this principle: our faith demands of us a certain sparingness in use, and the Church is obliged to live and to administer its own goods in such a way that the Gospel is proclaimed to the poor. If instead the Church appears to be among the rich and powerful of this world its credibility is diminished (*The Practice of Justice*, Rome 1971).

The credibility of our witness is not the only thing at risk if we allow ourselves to indulge in a high standard of living. Such a lifestyle can also rob us of that joy and happiness which rightfully belong to us, here and now, as followers of Jesus, the Christ.

Once, en route home from Ethiopia, I had to stop over in one of the European capitals. As it was a Saturday evening I went to Mass in the local parish. The church was a relatively new building, very large and extremely well kept, with good heat and light and many fine works of art, some old, some new, decorating the walls. Equal care had gone into the preparation of the liturgy, which was celebrated according to the norms of the Second Vatican Council. A choir of thirty to forty young people led the singing. Many young families were among the congregation, all of whom looked quite well heeled. But despite all this effort, which I greatly admired, there were two things which I found lacking: there was little sense of community and little sense of happiness among the congregation. There were few, if indeed any, smiles to be seen in that church.

I doubt whether this would have been so obvious to me had I not, only two days previously, taken part in a most joyful celebration of Mass with Christians in an isolated area of Ethiopia. The contrast could hardly have been more extreme. On that occasion our church had been no more than a tin hut with a makeshift table serving as an altar. All the two hundred people there were poorly dressed, and many were undernourished. They had come from different villages, some even from different tribal groups. I could nevertheless sense that, within the walls of that hut, a real community had gathered in worship. The Mass was a truly joyful celebration of a faith that was being lived out under very difficult political and social circumstances. A poor, destitute, and unjustly forgotten people have found in their faith a real sense of joy and happiness, which I fear we, in the more affluent West, have more or less lost.

The Book of Deuteronomy describes the contrast between the way in which God's people lived their faith in the desert and what happened once they began to enjoy the wealth of the

Promised Land. We are told that Moses lamented that once the people had grown rich they had also grown rebellious, that once they were fat and stuffed with food they abandoned God (cf. Deut 32:15). There is an uncomfortable similarity between that experience and our own today. Christians in the affluent societies of the West have not abandoned God, but by reaching a compromise with wealth they risk becoming distracted and tired in their response to him. The result is a faith that is joyless in its expression. The young churches of Ethiopia and elsewhere can teach us to rediscover the importance of that radical call to simplicity in lifestyle which is essential for anyone who is seeking a faith that will bring with it, here and now, a real sense of happiness.

CHAPTER 5

An Indispensable Role

You are salt for the earth. . . . You must, therefore, set no bounds to your love, just as your heavenly Father sets none to his.

—Matt 5:13-48

We will understand the real significance of Jesus' words, "You are the salt for the earth," only when we appreciate that salt was so vital for the preservation and flavoring of food that Matthew's community would have been unable to contemplate life without it. Jesus used this image to emphasize the indispensable role his followers were to play in relation to the wider community. He made clear that their faith was not to be divorced from their everyday lives, that it was to be more than just "we believe." Faith was a gift to be shared. They had been called essentially for the sake of others, and consequently their lives were not to be self-centered or lived in a way that would allow them to ignore what was going on around them. Their belief in Jesus as the Messiah demanded active involvement in the lives of others. "No one lights a lamp to put it under a tub; they put it on the lampstand where it shines for everyone in the house" (v. 15). By word and by example, Jesus' followers were to reflect the true nature of God's love. But they would only do so as long as they did not lose sight of their own identity: salt that loses its taste, Jesus warned, is good for nothing.

Matthew recognized that those who embraced this new way of life would need more than a set of new rules to govern their behavior. So he collected together those sayings of Jesus which had given his community a completely new insight into the nature of God's love. This insight was to be the inspiration for their own behavior, encouraging them to become more fully involved in their neighbors' lives and helping them avoid the danger of losing sight of their own identity.

Jesus' teaching was, of course, rooted in the Law and the prophets. From the Book of Leviticus they would already have grasped that the way we treat others affects our relationship with God; the command "Love your neighbor as yourself" (19:18) clearly prohibited revenge and the bearing of grudges. The prophets, too, had emphasized the link between true worship of God and genuine love of neighbor. Isaiah had warned that God could not "endure solemnity combined with guilt" (1:13). Their outstretched hands would attract God's attention only insofar as they also learned "to do good, search for justice, discipline the violent, be just to the orphan, plead for the widow" (Isa 1:14-17).

However, the love of neighbor preached in the Old Testament was restricted to members of one's own tribal community and to those strangers who had chosen to live within it. People were not expected to look beyond its boundaries, and they were certainly under no obligation to love their enemies.

The love Jesus required from his followers was, by contrast, unconditional; it could not be confined to kith and kin, nor did it depend upon how others behaved toward them. "You must, therefore, set no bounds to your love, just as your heavenly Father sets none to his" (v. 48). The norm for their loving was to be nothing other than the love of God himself. The way in which God relates was to become the prototype for all human relationships. This new awareness called for a radical change of outlook, in which they would have to begin by redefining what they meant by "neighbor," since Jesus was clearly asking them to embrace those who were previously considered unacceptable.

Matthew was no armchair theorist. He lived in a world where oppression and injustice were an accepted part of life. His own community, having seen Jesus meet with a violent and unjust death, were already beginning to experience direct opposition from the established religious leaders and civil authorities. He was sufficiently in touch with the raw realities of life to appreciate that, since their faith did not permit them to cut themselves off from others, they would have to enter a world where human conflict was part of everyday experience. Murder, adultery, divorce, retaliation, mistrust, hatred—these were the sorts of problems his community would have to tackle, with Jesus' own words and example as their guide.

Jesus had shown how it was possible to practice God's way of loving in a world which was adrift from God. Feelings of anger, lust, fear, the desire to dominate or to misuse others, resentment and revenge, all could be overcome by a genuine desire to live reconciled with everyone, good and bad alike. Those who strive to live in this way reflect God's openness to all his creatures. "Your light must shine in people's sight so that, seeing your good works, they may give praise to your Father in heaven" (5:16).

In practice this meant that the disciples were to offer no resistance to the wicked, to love their enemies, and to pray for those who persecuted them. Matthew was echoing the message of the Beatitudes: the follower of Jesus the Messiah has no need to defend his or her rights with force. Like wealth and social esteem, recourse to violence is a real obstacle in the search for a mature faith. On the other hand, experience of the vulnerability of the defenseless not only helps to reinforce people's sense of their human incompleteness and so of their need for God, it also gives them an opportunity to bear public witness to their complete trust in God's presence. For Matthew, the whole process of growing in faith depended upon the disciple's willingness to root the whole of his or her life in God, to learn to renounce self: "Anyone who does not take his cross and follow in my footsteps is not worthy of me" (Matt 10:38). Jesus himself had become the new standard. He was the true example of a human life fully rooted in God, and he pointed the disciples in the direction they were to follow. It was by their own wholehearted acceptance of his way that his followers were called to transform human society.

Matthew pinpointed at least some of the problems the followers of Jesus would have to face, and he indicated that a new spiritual outlook was essential if they were to survive their encounter with an unjust and divided world. But he offered no guidance on points of detail, nothing to help people through the dilemmas to which this new way of living would inevitably give rise. This means that succeeding generations of Christians have interpreted the Sermon on the Mount in a variety of ways.

For example, early Christian literature suggests that for at least the first three centuries Christians took a strongly pacifist position on questions of war and violence. Writers like Justin the Martyr, Tertullian, and Origen upheld the principle of nonviolence as the only way in which a Christian could fulfill the expectations of the Sermon on the Mount. They clearly believed that Christians had a responsibility to realize in their own lives the vision of Isaiah, who proclaimed: "They will hammer their swords into ploughshares and their spears into sickles. Nation will not lift sword against nation, no longer will they learn how to make war" (Isa 2:4). For them the issue was clear: no Christian could take part in armed conflict and still maintain the witness he or she had been called to give; the sword had no place in the life of a Christian—though we cannot be sure how widely this belief was held. There is evidence to suggest that during these centuries some Christians, at least, were involved in military service.

With Constantine's acceptance of Christianity as the religion of the Roman Empire came a notable change of attitude. The predominantly pacifist outlook gradually gave way to an alternative vision, which accepted violence and war as legitimate under certain conditions. Great Christian leaders such as Ambrose and Augustine sincerely believed that in certain circumstances it was legitimate to take up the sword in the defense of justice or to establish peace.

As a result, it became difficult to distinguish the interests of the Church from those of the State, and through the ages Christians have been encouraged to participate in all sorts of wars, on the grounds that they have a moral responsibility to do so. The use of violence became an acceptable way of fulfilling the command "to love your neighbor as yourself." But although the effects of Constantine's conversion undoubtedly overshadowed the pacifist tradition of the early Church, it never disappeared entirely. In every generation a few Christians have firmly held on to what they believed to be the nonviolent principles of the Sermon on the Mount as the only legitimate way to approach conflict.

Matthew's Sermon on the Mount has often been described as an "impracticable ideal." There was even a time when it was regarded as a rule of life suitable only for monks. Fortunately, not all Christians took this point of view. Examples can be found throughout history of people who actually tried to put this "impracticable ideal" into practice, and who did so with remarkable success. Given the divided state of the world we live in, I find the witness of three such people particularly relevant today.

The world in which Francis of Assisi lived eight hundred years ago was equally marred by division—relations between the various parties to the conflict in the Lebanon today can give us some idea of the fear, contempt, and hatred which Christians and Muslims had for one another at that time. Their armies had been locked in battle for many years. Francis, a man of deep faith and compassion, felt obliged to make some practical attempt to heal the divisions. He was determined to cross the dividing line in the hope of meeting the Sultan and opening up some form of dialogue. When he made public his intentions, his supporters were deeply embarrassed. The authorities condemned his plan as immoral, since he would risk certain death.

Francis disregarded these reactions and set out with a companion on his peace mission. He was soon taken prisoner and brought before the Sultan, who had been advised not to listen to him but to have him put to death immediately. When Francis explained the reason for his visit and that he had come not as an envoy from the Christian camp but as a messenger from the God of compassion, the Sultan ignored his advisers and spent several days in discussion with him.

Francis did not succeed in stopping the conflict immediately. Nevertheless, his goodness and sincerity made such a deep impression on the Sultan that he and his companion were given not only their freedom but also the future right of safe-conduct in Muslim-held territories.

This episode from the life of Francis of Assisi shows how effective human compassion can be when inspired by faith, in breaking down barriers, in overcoming hostility, and in gaining trust. Faith always carries with it the seeds of hope; it calls for a readiness to put oneself out, and even at risk, for the sake of others. The experience of human vulnerability had taught Francis the importance of rooting the whole of his life in God. It was not Francis' faith which failed; the failure was on the part of those Christians who were not prepared to follow his example.

Pierre Theas lived in a Europe torn apart by war. He was a Frenchman, a Catholic bishop, imprisoned by the Germans toward the end of World War II because he had the courage to protest against the deportation of Jews. In the prison at Toulouse he took every opportunity to share his faith in the gospel with his fellow inmates, many of whom were French army officers. The gospel, he reminded them, called for the forgiveness of enemies. At first this message met with staunch resistance. One officer shouted at him: "The SS have killed my six sons; I'll never forget that." Although his fellow prisoners found the bishop's message difficult, one evening they invited him to pray with them the "Our Father" (Matt 6:9-13). They began their prayer in a hesitant and stammering manner, and by the time they had reached the words "as we forgive . . ." they suddenly faltered. Bishop Theas simply added the words "Germans." The men returned to their cells that night in silence.

Pierre Theas realized how difficult it was for them to accept the message of forgiveness. For centuries rivalry and bloodshed had marred the relationship between the two nations, and all these men belonged to a generation of Frenchmen which had been brought up to believe that "the Germans and the French are hereditary enemies." But that night in his prison cell, he felt liberated. He had been able to pray for his enemies from his heart. He decided that from then on he would dedicate his life to work for a Franco-German reconciliation, based on the spirit of the gospel which he had preached to his fellow prisoners.

Soon after the war, Theas met with others who shared his belief in the need to work for reconciliation. Through a program of study, prayer, and action they dedicated themselves to work together for peace, Christ's peace. Today the spirit of Pierre Theas lives on in the Pax Christi International Movement, which brings together thousands of people from many different nations who dedicate their lives to the difficult task of working for genuine reconciliation between nations. Like Matthew, Pierre Theas was no armchair theorist. He found the courage to act in a way that would not be expected of any man who had to face the indignities and insecurity of a prison cell.

Maria is a psychologist and the mother of ten children. The government of the state in which she lives vehemently opposes the spread of religion. She and her husband were outspoken in their criticism of its policies, and as a result both lost their jobs. The husband was eventually imprisoned, and the police spent several days searching the family home in the hope that they would find sufficient evidence to incriminate him. It was after one such search that Maria wrote to her friends:

> We are now really experiencing a hand-to-mouth existence. We have lost all our money, our security, our typewriter and many of our books. In spite of all this we experience now, more than ever, the joy of the presence of Christ. Our hearts are filled with peace and quiet. We know and believe he will not allow us to go hungry. He has human instruments through whom he will console and help us. Some of our friends cannot understand that in Christ we have much more than material security, and that our life in the Spirit gives us a true freedom, which is independent of physical confinement. We see values which come to us from the knowledge that God is always with us and he will not abandon us, in prison, in suffering, in trials. We are experiencing more than ever the reality of his presence. It is from this that we gain

our inner freedom, which enables us to love our enemies. This love cannot be broken; we only wish our enemies could experience this same love. Pray with us for our opponents who persecute us. Our whole family prays for them. It is possible that this is the purpose behind our sufferings and difficulties, for they need prayers more than we do.

Maria's letter provides us with the present-day testimony of someone who, at a moment of great vulnerability in her life, has found the strength to embrace the new standard of behavior called for in Matthew's Gospel.

These lives—of a mendicant friar, a diocesan bishop, and a working mother—have little in common, apart from a deep conviction that the gospel really does oblige us not to seek revenge but to love our enemies and to pray for those who persecute us. All three found sufficient courage to step outside the accepted norms of behavior in their respective societies. Their witness should compel other Christians to reexamine any attempt to dismiss the challenge of the Sermon on the Mount as an impracticable ideal.

Matthew's faith put him in the way of problems. Jesus used the analogies of salt and light to illustrate the role of the disciples because he wanted them to see the importance of being involved at every level of human existence. Christians were not to ignore the problems that come from living in an imperfect world. On the contrary, they were to learn to cope with them in ways that would reflect the truth that the unrestricted love of God is the only force which can check evil. Their task was hampered by the reality of sin in the world—not least their own innate selfishness, which made them put their own interests first. They would have found it impossible to relate to their neighbor in this radically new way, had they not first learned to respond to the challenge of the Beatitudes by putting their complete trust in God.

Christians have always had a tendency to be piecemeal in their approach to, and application of, the gospel—the Sermon on the Mount in particular. This is most noticeable today, when some who argue vehemently against adultery and divorce at the same time support the call for capital punishment and a policy of nuclear deterrence, which is based on the threat of massive retaliation against any would-be aggressor. The inconsistency does not seem to bother them. It does, however, take from the credibility of the gospel as a whole. Christians who want to promote what Matthew teaches about adultery and divorce must have the integrity to examine their attitudes toward the punishment of criminals and the nuclear defense policy.

When Ambrose and Augustine gave conditional assent to the use of the sword, they could never have imagined how the arms race would develop. Faced with today's sophisticated weapons, which are capable of such swift retaliation and massive destruction, humanity should surely be searching for new ways of dealing with conflict. Jesus' own words to Peter, ''Put your sword back, for all who draw the sword will die by the sword'' (Matt 26:52), are particularly pointed today.

The Second Vatican Council unequivocally and unhesitatingly condemned the use of nuclear weapons. It also recognized the urgent need for ''new approaches based on reformed attitudes'' (*Constitution on the Church in the Modern World*, par. 80). Nuclear weapons present such a threat to the survival of human life that the world may have no alternative but to embrace wholeheartedly Matthew's message of nonviolence. No matter how impracticable it may seem at first, nonviolence, as a basic principle in resolving conflict, needs to be given a chance. The example of the hundreds of thousands of people who crowded unarmed into the streets of Manila to face the military might of the Marcos regime shows how effective a nonviolent approach can be in bringing about real change. It is also a reminder that such an approach demands courage. The option for nonviolence does not allow one to run away from conflict; it simply obliges one to approach it in a different way. Gandhi caught the true spirit of the nonviolent approach when he said that it does not seek to overcome an enemy but rather to make an enemy a friend.

Jesus was making the same point when he told his followers: "If you are bringing your offering to the altar and there remember that your brother has something against you, leave your offering there before the altar, go and be reconciled with your brother first, and then come back and present your offering" (Matt 5:23-24). Jesus puts the obligation to seek reconciliation on his disciples; they must make the first move. Francis of Assisi, Pierre Theas, and Maria, the young mother—each in his or her own way—live up to that expectation. Their lives bear witness that faith can break down the barriers of fear, mistrust, and prejudice, all of which promote violence. If the world is to embrace the nonviolence of the gospel as a genuine alternative to military conflict, it will need many more people like these, prepared to lead the way by their own example.

The Sermon on the Mount, however one may want to interpret it, clearly calls for a close study of one's own attitudes, especially to others. A Christian should never be completely at home in the ways of the world. Followers of Jesus are called to live at all times in a way which reflects gospel values. If they are to do this effectively, their presence in society may need to be more disturbing than comforting.

CHAPTER 6

More Than an Outward Display

Be careful not to parade your uprightness in public to attract attention; otherwise you will lose all reward from your Father in heaven. . . .

—Matt 6:1-18

Matthew's Gospel was written primarily to help instruct Jewish converts to the Christian faith. All of them would have been familiar with the traditional Jewish practices of almsgiving, prayer, and fasting—in addition to observance of the law, these acts of piety were considered essential if a devout person was to keep his or her relationship with God on the right track. Matthew endorsed this view, but at the same time he warned against the risks inherent in such outward displays of piety. Almsgiving, fasting, and even prayer could easily be reduced to the level of mere performance, staged in order to impress onlookers. This was not at all what Jesus meant when he told his followers ''Your light must shine in people's sight, so that, seeing your good works, they may give praise to your Father in heaven'' (Matt 5:16). Far from encouraging them to seek popular recognition, he said they should avoid drawing attention to themselves. There was to be no pretense, no role playing in their lives, and nothing contrived to impress others.

Matthew's community would have been brought up on that spiritual advice which Tobit gave to his son, Tobias:

> Give your bread to those who are hungry, and your clothes to those who lack clothing. Of whatever you own in plenty, devote a proportion to almsgiving; and when you give alms do it ungrudgingly (Tob 4:16).

The problem was that, by the time of Jesus, the pious practice of almsgiving had acquired a ritual of its own, and the amount a person gave was read out in the synagogue. As a result people were tempted to give with an eye to publicity—the more they gave, the greater would be their reputation in the community. This meant that almsgiving was no longer fulfilling its true purpose.

The followers of Jesus had to rediscover that purpose by learning to give with no ulterior motive. They were not even to keep their own record of what they gave: "Your left hand must not know what your right is doing" (Matt 6:3). Almsgiving was meant to be spontaneous, a totally unself-conscious reaching out to those in need. It was a matter of putting the Golden Rule of the Gospel into practice: "So always treat others as you would like them to treat you" (Matt 7:12). Jesus taught them how important it was to divert attention from themselves and to focus on those in need—only when they had learned to do this effectively would their almsgiving enable them to sustain a true relationship with God.

Later on, Matthew described the scene of the Last Judgment, to show how important it is to learn to give spontaneously. God will reward with the gift of eternal life those who have learned to respond without calculation to the needs of their neighbors:

> "Lord, when did we see you hungry and feed you, or thirsty and give you drink? When did we see you a stranger and make you welcome, lacking in clothes and clothe you? When did we find you sick or in prison and go to see you?" And the King will answer, "In truth I tell you, insofar as you did this to one of the least of these brothers of mine, you did it to me" (Matt 25:37-41).

Prayer, too, was to be done without a thought for the approval of others. The disciples needed to have a deeper relationship with God than the ritualistic practices of the time would allow—and Jesus had made it clear that God was not interested in monologues. The true disciple would learn how to pray by opening up to God in the privacy of his or her heart. "Everyone who listens to these words of mine and acts on them will be like a sensible man who built his house on rock'' (Matt 7:24). This was to be the foundation of the disciple's relationship with God.

Of course Matthew was not ruling out the need for prayer in common (Matt 18:19-20); he was simply emphasizing that prayer is a dialogue with God and must be conducted from the heart. Matthew wanted his converts to realize that they could pray wherever they were. The effectiveness of their prayer did not depend on place or posture. What mattered was their attitude of mind and heart.

Such prayer called for trust: ''Your Father knows what you need before you ask him'' (Matt 6:8). It called for perseverance: ''Ask and it will be given to you; search, and you will find; knock, and the door will open to you'' (Matt 7:7). It called for faith: ''If you have faith everything you ask in prayer you will receive'' (Matt 21:22). Above all, it called for a willingness to forgive from the heart: ''Were you not bound to have pity on your fellow servant just as I had pity on you?'' (Matt 18:33). These were to be the hallmarks, indeed the prerequisites, for authentic prayer in Matthew's community.

There is a sense in which Matthew's entire Gospel could be considered a treatise on prayer. But he concentrates his message in a model prayer which he attributes to Jesus. By teaching his community to address God as ''Our Father in heaven'' he underlines at once the ''intimacy'' and the ''otherness'' of God in their lives. God is approachable by everyone, yet none can claim him exclusively as a personal or tribal deity, for ''his reign endures throughout all ages'' (Tob 13:1). Prayer is not a means of exerting pressure on God or keeping him under control; on the contrary, it is the means through which they will discover God's will and promote God's reign. It is important that they express their trust in God by asking him to provide for their daily needs. And it is equally important to ask God to forgive their failings— although Jesus pointed out that God's forgiveness would depend entirely on their willingness to forgive others.

''Yes, if you forgive others their failings, your heavenly Father will forgive you yours; but if you do not forgive others, your heavenly Father will not forgive your failings either'' (Matt 6:14-15).

Since Jesus had come not to abolish the Law but to fulfill it (Matt 5:17), he was surely referring to something more here than people's personal failings and the hurt they cause. We read in the Book of Deuteronomy that at the end of every seventh year all debts were to be cancelled: "You must remit whatever claim you have on your brother" (Deut 15:4). This called for openness of hand as well as openness of heart toward the poor. And Deuteronomy had a warning for those who, as the seventh year approached, were reluctant to give to those in need for fear that they would not be repaid: "Do not harden your heart or close your hand against that poor brother of yours; be openhanded with him and lend him enough for his needs" (Deut 15:8). Faith implies constant readiness to share one's good fortune, especially with those in need. So, while asking God's forgiveness for their own debts (Matt 6:12), the disciples were to respond to the needs of the oppressed and the poor in their midst. How should God listen to their cry for help if they remained deaf to the cry of others in need?

Matthew established an inseparable link between prayer and almsgiving. Prayer without almsgiving lacks authenticity, while almsgiving without prayer risks gaining nothing more than human approval. The disciple, open both to God and to his or her neighbor, learns to practice both of these acts of piety directly from the heart.

Although Jesus apparently did not encourage his disciples to fast (Matt 9:14), the practice was quickly taken up by the early Church, and Matthew's community would certainly have been familiar with it. The Law required a fast only on the Day of Atonement (Lev 16:31), but fasting gradually became the recognized sign of repentance, of a heart given totally to God. By Jesus' time, for many people it had become just another way of attracting attention. Matthew warned his converts against this urge to display one's piety in public. If that was their motive, their fasting would have no spiritual value. They were to learn to conceal their fasting, even making it look as if they were getting ready for a banquet (Matt 6:18). Only thus could they expect to attract God's attention.

Several centuries earlier, the prophet Isaiah had given a similar warning. His community were complaining that they were doing all their religious laws required—fasting, praying, and doing penance by dressing in sackcloth and ashes. Yet God seemed to acknowledge none of it: he was eluding them. "Why have we fasted, if you do not see; why mortify ourselves if you never notice?" (Isa 58:3). Isaiah's answer was unambiguous: God would take notice only when all this outward observance of ritual signified a real desire for change in their lives. What they needed to do, he told them, was to start acting justly. Once they were willing to let the oppressed go free, to share their bread with the hungry, to clothe the naked, and to shelter the homeless poor, they would find God in their lives. What was the point of fasting if, while doing so, they ignored a neighbor in need? To be of spiritual value their fast needed to go hand in hand with genuine and active concern for the needy. Fasting was never intended as a test of one's self-discipline; its purpose was to create an inner desire for God.

Almsgiving, prayer, and fasting were soon to become the mainstay of Christian spirituality. The season of Lent, a period of forty days preceding the Feast of Easter, was set aside as a time when the whole Church would make a particular effort to practice daily those traditional forms of piety. They were recognized as an effective way of renewing the total commitment which a Christian makes at baptism as the outward sign that a person is sincere in his or her efforts to repent.

The Bible uses the word "repent" to convey the idea of a complete turning round; repentance is an act in which the whole person is engaged—it involves the heart just as much as the mind and the body. God asks for nothing less. However, there is always the danger—as both Isaiah and Jesus recognized—that a person will respond to God's call on one level but not on the other. Sometimes people are aware of what they are doing, more often they are not.

When we use the word "hypocrite" today we normally mean that a person is consciously behaving falsely: the hypocrite is the one who pretends to be other, and even better, than he or she really is. In the Bible, however, the word does not necessarily imply conscious falseness in the person accused of hypocrisy. Hypocrites are assumed to be playing a role—in other words, putting on a public performance—but the fact that their heart is not fully in tune with their actions does not necessarily mean they are insincere, simply that they are misguided.

Matthew warned his followers to be aware of this possibility. For, whether they were conscious of their own insincerity or simply behaving in a misguided way, the effect would be the same: they would be out of touch with God. They would have failed to grasp the message of Jesus: "It is not anyone who says to me, 'Lord, Lord,' who will enter the Kingdom of Heaven, but the person who does the will of my Father in Heaven" (Matt 7:21).

Christians were soon to discover for themselves how easy it is to succumb to this temptation. Although Lent was supposed to be a time for sincere self-scrutiny, they found—as we do today—that their outward observance frequently failed to achieve its purpose of bringing them into closer touch with God. Not that this undermines the value of these traditional practices; it simply emphasizes the importance of developing a fully integrated spirituality. We cannot hope to experience the presence of God in any real way unless we are also willing to seek out our neighbor in need. Isaiah's message still holds good for us:

> Then you will cry for help and the Lord will answer; you will call and he will say, "I am here!" If you do away with the yoke, the clenched fist and the malicious words, if you deprive yourself for the hungry and satisfy the needs of the afflicted, your light will rise in the darkness, and your darkest hour will be like noon (Isa 58:9-10).

Any form of prayer or fasting which allows people to remain unaware of a neighbor in need has clearly lost touch with its biblical roots. Those whose experience of God is authentic will be more, not less, aware of their neighbor, and in their desire to share God's love will be glad to share that neighbor's pain. Today more than ever, Christian spirituality calls for active concern for the daily needs of one's neighbor, a concern that is rooted in heartfelt prayer and in a willingness to curb the natural urge to satisfy one's own needs and desires.

That means more than sitting at home waiting for a knock on the door. The Second Vatican Council reminded Christians of their duty to seek out those in need:

> Wherever people are to be found who are in want of food and drink, of clothing, housing, medicine, work, education, the means necessary for leading a truly human life; wherever there are people racked by misfortune or illness, people suffering exile or imprisonment, Christian charity should go in search of them and find them out, comfort them with devoted care, and give them the help that will relieve their needs. This obligation binds, first and foremost, the more affluent individual and nations (*Decree on the Apostolate of Lay People,* par. 8, ed. by Austin Flannery, O.P., Costello Publishing Company).

The Council set no limits to this search; it reminded believers that in an age of rapid communication "people in every part of the globe have become as members of a single family." True concern is sensitive to the freedom and dignity of those who need help—a sensitivity which the hypocrites condemned by Matthew lacked (Matt 6:2).

The Council also drew an important distinction between the demands of justice and those of charity. "The demands of justice must first be satisfied; that which is already due in justice is not to be offered as a gift of charity" (par. 8).

Sixteen hundred years ago, Augustine, the North African bishop of Hippo, was preaching a similar message. Since material goods are there to meet the basic needs of all human beings, Christians, he argued, should strictly limit what they own, keeping only what is necessary for life. Anything over and above basic food and clothing is superfluous, and we have no moral right to hold on to it. "The superfluities of the rich," he once wrote, "are necessities of the poor. When you possess superfluities you possess the goods of others" (Commentary on Ps 147). Indeed, Augustine felt so strongly about what he regarded as the Christian obligation to share that he considered failure to do so as equivalent to fraud. Although Vatican II was not quite so explicit, the basic principle remains: to give of what one has in excess is a matter of justice, to give of what one needs oneself is true Christian almsgiving. The demands of almsgiving are greater than those of justice.

Pope Paul VI reminds us that if, as Christians, we want to fulfill our moral responsibility for the poor, we will have to do more than express concern or give away what we do not really need: we will also have to reassess our own lifestyle. In his encyclical letter *The Progress of Peoples (Populorum Progressio),* Pope Paul claims that genuine love tries to uncover the causes of poverty and to find real and effective ways of overcoming them. We need continually to ask why people are poor and to question the social and economic structures of a world which allows so many millions to live and die in want.

One issue which calls for urgent analysis is that of interest rates on loans to the developing countries. When it was discovered that there were children among those who had been killed during the American bombing raid on Tripoli, people all over the world expressed their moral outrage. Yet, when they hear that interest rates have risen on loans to developing countries, those same people show little concern, even though the effects can be as devastating as those of bombing a city. Cardinal Paulo Evaristo Arns, archbishop of Sao Paulo, Brazil, put the matter quite simply when he said: "Every time the United States raises its interest rates, thousands die in the Third World, because money that could be used for health and food is sent outside."

If Christians in the rich nations of the world want to pray the "Our Father," and all that it implies, with sincerity, they should perhaps ask themselves whether it is possible to remain silent in a society which lives off the misfortunes of others—and whether they should not be in the forefront of the current debate on international debt. Many Third World countries are finding it extremely difficult to pay off even some of the interest that has accumulated on their international debts. Against this background, Jesus' words, "forgive us our debts as we forgive those who are in debt to us" (Matt 6:12), should be particularly challenging for those who already enjoy the good things of life.

But while it is true that Christians should develop a global understanding of the problems of the poor, they should also guard against a tendency to focus exclusively on the needs of the poor overseas. Misery and destitution hide so easily behind the respectable façades of our own cities. Active concern for the poor in Africa, Asia, and Latin America must be combined with an equally active concern for the oppressed and outcast members of our own society. It is much easier to write to one's member of Parliament [Congress] or even to sign a check in response to a famine appeal than, say, to accept a young unmarried mother into one's home—or at least to remain open to the possibility of doing so, for not everyone could cope psychologically with the emotional strain that such a close encounter would demand. A concern for one's neighbor in the global context that is not rooted in an awareness of and sensitivity to needs nearer home will lack authenticity. As will any act of voluntary fasting that is not combined with a genuine desire to act in solidarity with the two-thirds of the world's people who are obliged to fast simply because they do not have enough food.

In heartfelt prayer we begin with a humble acknowledgment of our human incompleteness and our need for God. We thank God for calling us into the partnership of life—in which he sustains and upholds us. We recognize that God is not a tame superbeing living totally apart from the world and intervening on demand to ensure success or protect the petitioner from some impending threat. Christian prayer happens the moment we become fully aware that God is present in the midst of human experience: "I am with you always; yes, to the end of time" (Matt 28:20).

CHAPTER 7

Jesus, a Man of Compassion

Suddenly a man with a virulent skin disease came up and bowed low in front of him, saying, "Lord, if you are willing, you can cleanse me." Jesus stretched out his hand and touched him saying, "I am willing. Be cleansed." And his skin disease was cleansed at once. . . .

—Matt 8:1-4

In the Hebrew tradition, sickness and disease were closely associated with sin. Those who suffered from contagious skin diseases were considered to be unclean and were subject to strict laws which excluded them from community life. The Book of Leviticus, the devout person's rule book, was firm on how such people should be treated:

Anyone with a contagious skin disease will wear torn clothing and disordered hair; and will cover the upper lip and shout, "Unclean, unclean." As long as the disease lasts, such a person will be unclean and, being unclean, will live alone and live outside the camp (Lev 13:45-46).

Once we realize this we can appreciate more fully just how extraordinary it was for Jesus to act in the way he did. Showing no regard for the accepted code of practice, he reached out and touched an untouchable. His compassion and his sincere concern for the isolated, lonely figure of the leper overruled all other considerations. He responded immediately to the poor man's cry for help: "Lord, if you are willing, you can cleanse me" (v. 3), and he acted without hesitation; he did not disappoint the trust and

51

the faith that had been placed in his power to heal. The story of the encounter with the leper gives a good insight into Jesus' human qualities.

But here as always, Matthew's main concern is to show that Jesus is the Messiah. He presents the miracles, the cures, and the authority over demons as external signs which helped to establish Jesus' true identity; they provided the necessary evidence that the messianic age had come. Isaiah had said, "On him will rest the spirit of Yahweh" (Isa 11:2). Jesus' actions were proof that the spirit, the power of God, was with him. Joel, too, had prophesied the outpouring of the spirit as the sign of the new age: "Even on slaves, men and women, shall I pour out my spirit in those days" (Joel 3:2). A leper (Matt 8:3), an army officer's servant (Matt 8:13), and an elderly bedridden woman (Matt 8:14-15) were among the first to experience, through their contact with Jesus, the outpouring of God's healing spirit. They were the living witnesses to Jesus' true identity. He was the Lord whom Matthew's community worshiped; people "bowed low in front of him" (Matt 8:2). This belief dominates the Gospel and overshadows any attention which Matthew gives to Jesus' human characteristics.

The various stories that Matthew relates in chapters eight to ten do, however, provide some important insights into the lifestyle and character of the historical Jesus. As Matthew follows Jesus through the early stages of his controversial mission, a model for the life of faith clearly begins to emerge.

Jesus was a man of compassion. He had time for people; he reached out to them in their need; he freed them from their disabilities and fears. He gave hope and new life to those who were racked by misfortune and grief: "Take comfort, my child, your sins are forgiven. . . . Get up, pick up your bed and go off home" (Matt 9:1-6). He was always ready to set aside his own plans in order to respond to the needs of others: "My daughter has just died, but come and lay your hand on her and her life will be saved" (Matt 9:19). He addressed himself to the problems of the crowds in general, and yet he was always aware of and sensitive to the needs of the individual, especially the weak:

"She was thinking, 'If only I can touch his cloak I shall be saved.' Jesus turned round and saw her and said to her, 'Courage, my daughter, your faith has saved you'" (Matt 9:21-22).

Jesus was always ready to engage in dialogue. He was not easily embarrassed by the unconventional behavior of others: "As Jesus went on his way, two blind men followed him shouting, 'Take pity on us, son of David.' . . . He said to them 'Do you believe I can do this?' They said, 'Lord, we do'" (Matt 9:27-28). He was not afraid to confront evil head on: "Two demoniacs came towards him out of the tombs—they were so dangerously violent that nobody could use that path" (Matt 9:28-34). Jesus did not sit at home waiting for people to come his way; he went out in search of people. His whole life was oriented toward others. He was always available, and especially to those in need.

Jesus was a man of faith, tough, uncompromising, singleminded, and totally absorbed in the mission, the work, which God the Father had given him: "They were astounded and said, 'Whatever kind of man is this, that even the winds and the sea obey him?'" (Matt 8:27). He was totally unconcerned about his own material comforts. He did not seek status or security by surrounding himself with personal wealth and possessions: "Foxes have holes and the birds of the air have nests, but the Son of man has nowhere to lay his head" (Matt 8:20). He was not particular about the company he kept and did not allow the opinions or expectations of others to inhibit him. He was not frightened to shock or disturb the religious minded: "When the Pharisees saw this, they said to his disciples, 'Why does your Master eat with tax collectors and sinners?'" (Matt 9:12). He did not feel obliged to encourage his followers to conform to the pious practices of others: "Then John's disciples came to him and said, 'Why is it that we and the Pharisees fast, but your disciples do not?'" (Matt 9:14). Jesus did not believe in compromise. He was unwilling to patch up what really needed to be changed: "No one puts a piece of unshrunken cloth onto an old cloak, because the patch pulls away from the cloak and the tear gets worse" (Matt 9:16). He was not frightened to confront the need for radical, structural changes. He recognized that a new spirit called for new forms of religious life, a completely new way of living. It was necessary to put "new wine in fresh skins" (Matt 9:17).

Jesus was not a loner. He actively sought the cooperation of others and called on the most unlikely of people to share in his life and work—a tax collector would have been looked upon as an unworthy and totally disreputable person (Matt 9:9). In other words, those who were considered by the religious leaders to be out of touch with God were the very people who found a new faith in the presence of Jesus. He taught them by word and example: he formed them into a community of believers. He shared with them his own authority and power (cf. Matt 10:1).

The practice of mercy was to be the distinguishing mark of the new community. "Go and learn the meaning of the words: Mercy is what pleases me, not sacrifice" (Matt 9:13). This, of course, had been one of the favorite themes of prophets such as Hosea and Amos. They taught that what pleases God above all else is a self-giving love expressed in a genuine daily care for others: "I do not look at your communion sacrifices of fat cattle. Spare me the din of your chanting . . . but let justice flow like water, and uprightness like a never-failing stream" (Amos 5:22-24).

Now Jesus was preaching the same message. And more than that, he was showing his disciples by his own example how to put it into practice, how to reach out toward those in spiritual and physical need. Their mercy, their practical day-to-day love, was to recognize no limits; it was not to be bound by the ritualistic codes which prohibited association with the so-called unclean. They, like Jesus, were to "cure the sick, raise the dead, cleanse those suffering from virulent skin diseases, drive out devils" (Matt 10:8).

This was a task, however, which demanded total commitment. There was no room for hesitation or a halfhearted effort: " 'Lord, let me go and bury my father first.' But Jesus said, 'Follow me, and leave the dead to bury their dead' " (Matt 8:21-22). Nor was any material advantage to be gained from this work. On the contrary, those who wanted to follow Jesus had to be prepared to give up their accustomed lifestyle and learn to put all their trust in God: "Provide yourselves with no gold or silver, not even with coppers for your purses, with no haversack for the journey or spare tunic or footwear or a staff . . ." (Matt 10:9-10). Experiencing the vulnerability of the poor, they would find security in their willingness to follow faithfully in the footsteps of Jesus.

But they would also have to expect the same sort of opposition that Jesus himself had to confront: "The disciple is not superior to the teacher" (Matt 10:24). Jesus had been wrongly accused and denounced by the Pharisees: "It is through the prince of devils that he drives out devils" (Matt 9:34). He had been misunderstood even by John the Baptist's disciples, who should have been more sympathetic to his life and work (cf. Matt 9:14ff.). He had been rejected by a whole city of people, who were frightened by his presence and "implored him to leave their neighborhood" (Matt 8:34). Some of those whom he had helped ignored his wishes: "Then Jesus sternly warned them, 'Take care that no one learns about this.' But when they had gone away they talked about him all over the countryside" (Matt 9:30-31).

Yet despite all these setbacks, Jesus was not discouraged from carrying out the mission entrusted to him by God the Father, and the disciples had to show the same singlemindedness in their own pursuit of God's work. Their efforts were not to depend on the response of others to their message. They had to learn to persevere in their task: "And if anyone does not welcome you or listen to what you have to say, as you walk out of the house or town shake the dust from your feet" (Matt 10:14). They had no time to be distracted by personal hurts that came from rejection. Their duty was to move on.

The mission which Jesus entrusted to his newly formed community called for the same sort of courage that he himself had demonstrated: they had to learn to carry the message of Jesus the Messiah without fear. "Why, every hair on your head has been counted. So there is no need to be afraid" (Matt 10:31). God's Spirit dwelling within them would provide them with the necessary strength to fulfill this task (cf. Matt 10:20).

But Matthew warned his community that at times their faith would indeed be tested. His account of how Jesus calmed the storm at the request of the disciples, who were afraid for their lives, was a salutary reminder that even their faith could fail at times of crisis. Only prayer would sustain the community in its missionary efforts. They would do well to make their own the prayer of the disciples in the boat: "Save us, Lord, we are lost!" (Matt 8:23-27).

The faith of Jesus, as manifested in Matthew's Gospel, is outgoing and active. It is motivated by the example of God's own mercy. It reaches out to embrace the needy, and expresses itself in a genuine, practical day-to-day concern for others. It is a faith which brings people into communion not only with God but also with one another. It breaks down human barriers, drawing people out of their isolation and teaching them to discover the beauty of life in community. It is a faith which has the power to heal, to enable broken, hurt human beings to find wholeness in their lives. It gives new meaning, a new sense of purpose to life—without, it should be said, holding out any false hopes or promises: it is rooted in reality, and it offers no material advantages. The faith manifested by Jesus calls for nothing less than total commitment to God and total involvement in the lives of others.

When Jesus said to Matthew, the tax collector, "Follow me" (Matt 9:9), he challenged him to choose between his old lifestyle and the new way of faith. Matthew's choice necessitated fundamental changes in his way of living. He had to learn to reinterpret the whole of his experience. He had to give up many of the things that he had previously valued and to set aside the natural tendency to seek security through the accumulation of wealth and possessions. He was not to try to accommodate his old ambitions within his new lifestyle. Jesus was calling him to be a pilgrim on the road of faith. He was to witness to God's values by his actions and lifestyle as well as by his words. "No one can be the slave of two masters: he will either hate the first and love the second, or be attached to the first and despise the second.

You cannot be the slave of both God and money'' (Matt 7:24).

Matthew's community had to learn to make the same choice. Faith required that they find their security in their vocation; there could be no compromise with their old way of living. And faith makes the same demands today. Christians are called to make a fundamental option to live as Jesus lived and taught others to live, to witness by word and example to God's values.

The effect that this option will have on their lifestyle is not as clear cut today as it was for Matthew's community, who did not have the worries that property and other possessions have brought into the life of the Church, particularly in the West. After Constantine's conversion, when the Roman State embraced the Christian faith, it became more difficult for Christians to develop the distinctive lifestyle which would enable them to carry out effectively the mission entrusted to them by Jesus Christ. The temptation was to adapt his example of faith to the social structures and expectations of a so-called Christian society. And that temptation in one guise or another has plagued the Christian Church throughout the centuries. Christians soon discover how easy it is to forget Jesus' warnings: ''No one puts a piece of unshrunken cloth into an old cloak . . . nor do people put new wine into old wineskins'' (Matt 9:17). Jesus gives his followers a new spirit, and this calls for a totally new way of living. Any attempt to compromise the Christian faith can have disastrous consequences.

This is only too true today. The idea of investing large sums of money to ensure the future material well being of the Church as an institution would have been totally foreign to the mind of Matthew's community (cf. Matt 10:9-10). Yet the Western Church holds on to collective material wealth which has a clearly adverse effect on its ability to give distinctive and unambiguous witness to the spiritual and eternal values of the gospel. It has certainly made it more difficult for the individual Christian to decide between what is and what is not an appropriate lifestyle for effective witness.

Property and wealth bring with them the cares and anxieties which can easily distract the Christian community from its God-given mission. Once life becomes cluttered with possessions there is always the risk that individuals and communities will give way to the natural tendency to stand still and build protective barriers around what one owns. In such circumstances it is easy for a Christian to lose sight of the fact that faith is essentially a call to keep moving onward to be a pilgrim. God told Abraham: ''Leave your country, your kindred and your father's house for a country which I shall show you'' (Gen 11:1). Abraham responded wholeheartedly to God's promptings, setting out into the unknown in search of a fuller life. Faith makes the same demand on the Christian today. It calls for detachment from material wealth and social structures—concern about property and status so easily gets in the way of one's ability to reach out to others, especially to the needy.

Compared with the Church of the poor in countries like Ethiopia or Brazil, the Western Church looks tired and weary, overburdened as it is with the cares of ownership and wealth. If it is to rediscover the vitality so essential to effective mission, the Church in Europe and North America may well have to shed much of its accumulated wealth.

But the Western Church will not be spurred on to meet this challenge simply by the witness of the Church in the poorer nations of the world. It will also have to be led by the example of its own individual members. Bishops, priests, religious, and laity need carefully to scrutinize their own lifestyles—as the 1971 Synod of Bishops recognized when it proclaimed that the Church cannot afford to be two-faced about temporal possessions.

The Church must learn to live its life and to administer property in such a way that it does not compromise the preaching of the gospel. And the individual Christian must be free to respond to the needs of others; too much attachment to possessions can seriously restrict that freedom and make Christian witness less credible. Lifestyle is a crucial matter for the Christian: where it does not facilitate mission it inevitably hinders it.

A genuine willingness to associate with the poor and the needy and with those whom society has overlooked and forgotten is another essential quality of Christian life. Jesus showed by words and example how God gives preferential attention to the neglected and the marginalized in society. He instructed his followers to seek them out, to heal their wounds, and to bring them back into community (cf. Matt 10:8). The Second Vatican Council declared that every Christian has "an inescapable duty" to reach out in care for a neighbor in need (cf. *Decree on the Apostolate of Lay People,* par. 8). Openness to others combined with real sensitivity to their needs and willingness to share one's time and material goods remain the essential qualities which today's disciple needs to develop in response to the words of Jesus Christ: "Follow me" (Matt 9:9).

CHAPTER 8

Challenge More than Comfort

It was Peter who answered, "Lord," he said, "if it is you, tell me to come to you across the water." Jesus said, "Come." Then Peter got out of the boat and started walking towards Jesus, across the water, but noticing the wind, he took fright and began to sink. "Lord," he said, "Save me!" Jesus put out his hand at once and held him.

—Matt 14:28-31

Matthew's Gospel is more than a biography of Jesus; it is the story of a young Church's growth in faith. His community believed in Jesus as the risen Lord, and he was anxious to help them consolidate their faith. Belief in the resurrection permeates his account of what Jesus said and did, and his story of the disciples' encounter with Jesus in the midst of a storm at sea reflects his understanding of the relationship between the risen Christ and his Church community. Ben Sira, author of the Book of Ecclesiasticus, spoke of "Wisdom" passing over the waves of the sea in search of rest and somewhere to "pitch camp" (cf. Sir 24:6-7). Jesus, God's Word made flesh, chose the Church, symbolized by the group of the disciples in the boat, as his dwelling place (cf. John 1:14). "The men in the boat bowed down before him and said, 'Truly, you are the son of God' " (Matt 14:33).

The community firmly believed that Jesus was the Messiah, but like the disciples in the boat, they were soon to discover how easy it was, especially when the going got rough, to lose confidence in him. Peter and the other disciples panicked in a time of crisis. Yet the Lord came to them; he reached out to them in their moment of need. Their lack of faith was not an obstacle to God's love. Whatever the circumstances, the community had to learn to put their complete trust in the power of Jesus, their risen Lord. "I am with you always; yes, to the end of time" (Matt 28:20).

Matthew offers us here a wonderful insight into the nature of faith and into how God relates to people. The Book of Genesis describes how Adam, after his sin of disobedience, took fright when he "heard the sound of the Lord God walking in the garden," and hid himself among the trees. God came in search of him—"Where are you?" he asked (Gen 3:9)—and the rest of the Old Testament unfolds the story of God's search.

Then, in Jesus, God and man were brought face to face again. Through him people were able to rediscover their true relationship with God. He helped them to understand that it was God who was seeking human company, God who was reaching out to embrace the human person, God who had found his way into the midst of our human confusion. So Peter, unlike Adam, did not feel that he had to hide his face in shame. In his moment of failure, he was able to look directly at Jesus and cry out, "Lord, save me!" (Matt 14:31).

Jesus' invitation to Peter to come to him across the water echoes the call of Abraham, who was commanded by God to leave behind the security of his father's house (Gen 12:2). "It was by faith that Abraham obeyed the call to set out for a country that was the inheritance given to him and his descendants, and that he set out without knowing where he was going" (Heb 11:8). Both men quickly discovered that faith can be more of a challenge than a source of comfort in life. God frequently expects us to forgo our natural desire to work within a secure and well-ordered structure. At times faith can make demands which appear to us to be totally unreasonable. But "anyone who finds his life will lose it; anyone who loses his life for my sake will find it" (Matt 10:39). Risk taking is essential to faith.

The story of Peter's failure was important to Matthew's community. After all, he was the rock chosen by Jesus to be the foundation of the new community: "You are Peter, and on this rock I will build my community. And the gates of the underworld can never overpower it" (Matt 16:18). Peter was an impulsive man. His heart, rather than his head, tended to govern his actions. The very sight of Jesus provoked an immediate response: he felt that he had to prove his faith. " 'Lord,' he said, 'if it is you, tell me to come to you across the water' " (14:28). When Jesus took him at his word, and said, "Come," Peter suddenly realized the risk involved. He was so gripped by fear that he almost lost sight of Jesus. He was going under.

The message for the community was clear. If this could happen to Peter, the very person to whom the risen Jesus had entrusted the well being of his new community (cf. John 21:15-17), it could also happen to them. But they were not to lose heart. It was only when Peter came face to face with failure that he fully acknowledged his need for God's help. This experience taught him that faith is a call to partnership with God, who asks for nothing less than total trust.

Nor were they to be put off at the thought of their own failure. Peter's experience should help them to value moments of crisis as an opportunity for growth in the life of faith. Matthew had already warned them that they could not expect to find real comfort in faith unless they were first prepared to accept its challenge. "Shoulder my yoke and learn from me, for I am gentle and humble in heart, and you will find rest for your souls" (Matt 11:29). Jesus' simple invitation "Come to me" (Matt 11:28) required total submission to his way.

Peter's experience taught them how important it was to keep Jesus continually in focus, allowing him to harness their emotions and their impulsive ways. If they did not, they would inevitably experience the same feeling of being pulled in opposite directions. Anxiety, doubt, fear, and confusion would blur their vision. They should have no fear, however, of the yoke of Jesus; he had not come to oppress: "Yes, my yoke is easy and my burden light" (Matt 11:30). Jesus was the servant of whom Isaiah had spoken; he had been "sent to bring the news to the afflicted, to soothe the broken-hearted, to proclaim liberty to captives, release those in prison. . ." (Isa 61:1-2). He would uphold them in the time of crisis: "Courage! It is I! Don't be afraid" (Matt 14:28).

The story of faith, from Abraham to Peter, always involved an element of risk. Those whom God called often felt that they were personally inadequate. Moses was convinced that he was not eloquent enough to do what God was asking: "Why should Pharaoh take any notice of a poor speaker like me?" he asked (Exod 6:12). Isaiah felt totally unworthy of his mission: "I am a man of unclean lips and I live among a people of unclean lips," he protested (Isa 6:5). Jeremiah believed that God had made a wrong choice: "You see, I do not know how to speak: I am only a child!" he replied (Jer 1:6). Hosea, instructed by God to choose a wife whom he knew would be unfaithful, had to learn from painful experience that God remains constant in his love, despite his people's unfaithfulness (cf. Hos 1:2-4). And Peter, too, felt unworthy of his vocation: "Leave me Lord, I am a sinful man," was his initial response to Jesus' call (Luke 5:8). Only when they accepted the challenge did they realize that God was in fact calling them into partnership. God himself was to be their companion on the journey of faith, their partner in accomplishing the task they had been chosen to undertake.

St. Paul had no doubts about the close relationship that exists between Jesus Christ and those who have been called to faith. In his Letter to the Romans he asked: "Can anything cut us off from the love of Christ—can hardships or distress, or persecution, or lack of food and clothing, or threats, or violence . . . ?" "No," was his reply, "we come through all these things triumphantly victorious, by the power of him who loved us" (Rom 8:35-37). Peter's experience on the stormy waters of the Galilean sea bore concrete witness to this power of Jesus Christ in the lives of those who accept his call. Matthew was reassuring his community: no matter how inadequate they personally might feel, they too would receive the help they needed in order to cope. A heartfelt prayer in the moment of crisis, and they would experience the grip of the outstretched hand that had saved Peter. Faith called for total trust.

When I examine some of my own inadequacies, doubts, and fears, I sometimes wonder whether God did not perhaps get it wrong when he invited me to set out on the journey of faith. I realize that this is a dangerous line of thought—it can so quickly become an excuse for not trying to meet the challenges that faith presents me with. But once I start seeing myself as second-league material, I am more likely to make compromises in my response to God's call. My life can become so cluttered with unnecessary possessions and my time so taken up in the pursuit of trivial matters that I sometimes begin to lose my overall sense of purpose and mission. I then find myself drifting along from day to day, living partly in the hope that tomorrow God will make his presence more obvious in my life and partly in the hope that he will not come looking for me, asking the same uncomfortable question he put to Adam, "Where are you?" (Gen 3:9). The honest answer frequently requires a radical change of direction, and that frightens me. I am often tempted to avoid putting the question to myself, simply out of fear that I may not be able to cope with the answer. And I suspect I am not alone in this experience.

It is easy for a believer to pay lip service to the idea of vulnerability as an essential experience of faith, while at the same time drifting along in life with a foot in both camps. We can profess our firm belief in Jesus and still find ourselves seeking all the comforts and security that secular society has to offer. The consequence of trying to take two directions at once can be as disastrous as meeting a storm at sea. Matthew's word for "doubt" conveys the same idea: it simply means double thinking, and it led to a crisis in Peter's life. The compromises we are tempted to make today inevitably lead to similar crises. Double thinking leads us into the wrong sort of risk taking, and losing sight of Jesus, we sink in the sea of today's materialism.

Fear of failure can be every bit as inhibiting as fear of change. The Christian must learn to be continually open, ready to recognize the risen Jesus when he or she least expects him, and through the most extraordinary circumstances of life. " 'Lord, when did we see you hungry or thirsty, a stranger or lacking clothes, sick, or in prison and did not come to your help?' Then he will answer, 'In truth I tell you, insofar as you neglected to do this to one of the least of these, you neglected to do it to me' " (Matt 25:44-45).

So we must avoid the temptation to use the boat, the Church community, solely as a place of refuge. It is tempting to hide behind the structure and the ritual that have grown out of Christian practice over the centuries, to become so absorbed with internal Church life that we become totally oblivious of the chaos that may well exist round about us. For Matthew's message is that Jesus, the Lord of faith, is also to be found in the midst of that chaos.

Jesus' rebuke to Peter: "You have so little faith, why did you doubt?" (Matt 14:32) gives a further insight into the nature of Christian belief. Faith is a mystery that unfolds through the very experience of trying to live it. The initial step toward faith is not always the most difficult. Jesus' explanation of the parable of the sower (Matt 13:20ff.) is a good illustration of this. The real challenge which faces the Christian has to do with perseverance. We will persevere in the journey of faith only insofar as we learn from the example of Peter how to cope with the inevitable crises and failures that will come our way. " 'Lord,' he cried, 'save me!' " (Matt 14:30).

CHAPTER 9

"How Many Loaves Have You?"

Jesus called his disciples to him and said, "I feel sorry for all these people: they have been with me for three days now and have nothing to eat. I do not want to send them off hungry, or they might collapse on the way. . . . How many loaves have you?"

—Matt 15:32-38

Matthew gives two separate accounts of the miracle of the loaves (cf. Matt 14:13-21). Though the two differ in some details, most biblical commentators suspect that Matthew based both on a single incident in the life of Jesus. The setting in both accounts was a lonely, deserted place (15:33). Jesus took pity on the crowd: first he healed them and then he fed them.

Matthew was not concerned with the details of what happened. His main aim was to establish Jesus' true identity and authority and so justify his own community's belief in Jesus as the Messiah. Miracles were important to Matthew only insofar as they helped to prove that the power of God rested in Jesus. He was not interested in portraying Jesus as a wonder worker. Jesus himself had in any case rejected that role when he was confronted by the devil in the wilderness (see Matt 4:3): God's power had been entrusted to him for the sake of others and not for his own glory. It is not clear here, however, exactly how Jesus made use of this power to feed the hungry people who had followed him back into the wilderness. Was there a physical multiplication of loaves, or did Jesus, by his own example, inspire some of the crowd to share with the others what little food they may have had with them? Matthew does not say.

The Book of Exodus tells how Moses was expected to provide food for the people of Israel when they grew tired and weary in the desert (Exod 16). The prophet Elisha, during a famine, had only twenty barley loaves and a little grain to feed a hundred men, but "he served them: they ate and had some left over, as Yahweh had said" (2 Kgs 4:44). Both men were used by God as intermediaries to provide food when it was needed. Jesus follows in this tradition. Given the time and the place, it would have been easier to turn a blind eye to these people's hunger. But he did not. His response was immediate and practical: he gave them food. But food is a gift from God which people have to learn to share.

It is unusual for Matthew to draw attention to Jesus' human feelings. The first thing he tells us here is that Jesus "felt sorry" for the people, that he was motivated by a genuine concern for their plight. Jesus had withdrawn to a lonely place in order to get away from the crowds (see Matt 14:13). He had now received the news of John the Baptist's death and needed time to pray and reflect quietly in the company of his close friends. But when the crowds followed them he showed no resentment, nor did he protest that they had invaded his privacy. Innate compassion for the weary crowd prompted him to set aside his personal needs. Their plight called for immediate action, and he reached out to touch them, to heal them, and to feed them.

The disciples made practical objections—"Where, in a deserted place, could we get sufficient bread for such a large crowd to have enough to eat?" (v. 33)—but these Jesus brushed aside, trying instead to involve them, to get them to cooperate. "How many loaves have you?" (v. 34). He was teaching them to forget their own concerns and to reach out to those in greater need. Jesus demonstrated by his own example how much God cares for the hungry and that he expects those who follow him to do the same.

Matthew's description of how Jesus took bread, gave thanks, broke the bread, and gave it to his disciples here in the desert anticipated his account of the Last Supper (see Matt 26:26). Throughout his Gospel he encouraged his community not only to look back at their religious roots but also to understand what God was doing for them there and then. The miracle of the loaves gave them the opportunity to reflect on the true nature of their Eucharistic worship. In the Eucharist, he was telling them, God was reaching out to uphold and sustain them in their own hour of need. "But mercy is what pleases me, not sacrifice" (Matt 9:13). If God was reaching out to them, they would have to learn to reach out to others. Their worship should inspire them with a deep sense of mission and compassion.

The 1971 Synod of Bishops drew attention to the relationship between Eucharistic worship and active concern for the well being of others. The liturgy, it recalled, is at the heart of the Church's life. When Christians gather together as a community to give thanks to God, they are reminded of the essential unity of the human race. The Eucharist forms the community and places it at the service of humanity (cf. par. 58, *Justice in the World*). The blessing and breaking of the Eucharistic bread should inspire today's Christians with the same sense of mission and the same compassion that were so obvious in the life of Jesus.

The work of this Synod was inspired by the thought of Pope Paul VI. In 1967 he had written an encyclical letter on the Christian response to the problems of worldwide poverty (cf. ch. 6). Pope Paul recognized that the world urgently needed to develop a sense of moral responsibility for the needy, and by this he did not simply mean expressions of concern. Action was what was called for. People had to be prepared to reassess and, if necessary, to change their own lifestyles, so that the poor of the world got more than just leftovers of the more affluent nations. Paul VI's directness reflected the simplicity of Jesus' question to his disciples: "How many loaves have you?" (Matt 15:34). He believed that compassion demands openness and a willingness to share even one's own bread with the hungry (cf. Isa 58:7).

The challenge was not new to the Christian Church. In the third century St. Clement of Alexandria similarly challenged the wealthy. It is absurd, he claimed, that one person should live in luxury while so many others suffer in poverty. Clement did not believe that possessions and wealth are evil in themselves—they are, after all, given to us by God. What he did believe was that we discover their real God-given value only when we share them. To share one's goods is more than a matter of Christian charity, it is also a matter of social justice. Clement challenged the rich with the thought that it is much more reasonable to spend money on human beings than on gold and precious stones.

St. Leo the Great (d. 461) also urged wealthy Christians to flee from the "filthy leprosy of greed" and to use God's gifts with justice and wisdom. He believed that anyone who became rich at the expense of others should be punished by everlasting want.

Pope Paul quoted St. Ambrose, the great fourth-century bishop of Milan, who boldly instructed the rich on their duty toward the poor: "You are not making a gift of what is yours to the poor man, but you are giving him back what is his. You have been appropriating things that are meant to be for the common use of everyone. The earth belongs to everyone, not to the rich." The early Fathers of the Church believed that the right to private property is not absolute and unconditional; it may never be exercised to the detriment of the common good. Their message still holds good today. "No one may appropriate surplus goods solely for his own private use when others lack the bare necessities of life" *(Populorum Progressio,* par. 23).

People who live in the rich industrial countries of the North today can no longer plead ignorance of the inequalities that exist between peoples and nations. Television and radio have brought the problems of the poor into their living rooms, yet this increased awareness has not been matched by a corresponding increase in concern and action on behalf of the millions who live and die in poverty. Fearful of insecurity, people still hoard unnecessary wealth and possessions as they plan and invest for the future. And meanwhile thousands who cannot satisfy even their present needs die in want every day. Each of us should find this inhuman situation an affront to conscience.

Today an estimated four hundred and fifty million people

are suffering from the effects of starvation and malnutrition. Every day no fewer than forty thousand of the world's children die. These are facts which I am sure many people find deeply disturbing, yet they fail to arouse widespread action on behalf of the poor. A single case of child abuse in Britain can provoke a much greater degree of moral outrage. This, I suppose, is understandable; statistics never expose the human tragedy that lies behind them—something that was brought home to me in a very vivid way on my last visit to Ethiopia.

One afternoon I was visiting a clinic run by a group of missionary sisters in a very remote district. They took me to see a young orphan boy who had been brought in that same morning. The sister explained that he was suffering from tuberculosis and the effects of malnutrition. The child, wrapped in a blanket, was sitting on the ground outside the small hut—the clinic, of course, had no beds. "What is your name?" I asked him. "Narsee," he replied. "How old are you?" The child responded in a weak voice, "I'm seven." There was a short silence, then he looked at me with haunting eyes: "I want to live," he said. Within a few hours of our conversation, Narsee was dead. His words, "I want to live," have haunted me ever since. For me, Narsee had voiced the plea for life of all those thousands of children who die every day. In the light of this experience, statistics— for me at least—now carry a sharper message.

Bob Geldof, the charismatic instigator of the Live Aid appeal, succeeded in tapping an innate source of compassion in individuals of all ages and all walks of life. He looked at the famine which was stalking Africa and recognized the need for immediate action. He inspired all sorts of people to give generously, enabling them to unleash their spontaneous desire to help the starving, and their immediate response helped to save many lives.

But the poor need more than the compassion of isolated individuals. Their problem will not go away until the governments of the rich nations accept that they have a moral responsibility for the well being of all the peoples in the world and not just for their own nations. This responsibility stems from the fact that human life is a sacred gift, to be cherished and guarded everywhere. What is lacking in today's world is the political will to act in favor of the poor and the hungry.

Paul VI believed that the gospel places upon Christians the responsibility of helping all peoples to live and to act as "one human race"—of helping individuals and nations to develop a radically new outlook which will enable them to grow away from their narrow self-interest and to embrace the needy as sisters and brothers, wherever they are. The rich nations must be prepared to share with those less fortunate their knowledge and skills as well as their wealth and other resources. Vast areas of the earth are underdeveloped, and even unstable, simply for want of technical knowhow. Peoples must "begin to work together to build the common future of the human race" *(Populorum Progressio,* par. 43).

The world cannot hope to bridge the divide between the poor and the wealthy nations unless it looks also at the ideological gap between East and West. *Détente* and development go hand in hand. A genuine desire to promote development implies a willingness to reexamine the fears, the mistrust, and the prejudices which have kept the world divided for most of this century. "May the day come when international relationships will be characterized by respect and friendship, when mutual cooperation will be the hallmark of collaborative efforts, and when concerted effort for the betterment of all nations will be regarded as a duty by every nation" *(Populorum Progressio,* par. 65).

The joint operation, through which the RAF and the Soviet Air Force brought urgent food supplies to the more isolated areas of Ethiopia, offered a glimmer of hope for the future, but sadly this hope remains largely unfulfilled. One of the tasks facing Christians is to work for better relationships between the power blocs. The cry of the poor makes this not just a priority but a matter of urgency.

Emergency food aid cannot solve the chronic problems of the world's poor. Hunger is a symptom of a much deeper malaise. The early Fathers of the Church helped to identify this when they spoke of the need for justice. Paul VI claimed that genuine love compels people to uncover the causes of poverty and search for effective ways of overcoming them. Christians should continually be asking why so many people have to live and die in poverty when the Bible makes it quite clear that God never intended any human person, let alone a child, to suffer in this way. It is an uncomfortable question demanding a reassessment of one's whole way of life. It is always easier to give charity than to ask why people need it. People readily—and rightly—identify with Mother Teresa in her admirable efforts on behalf of the poor and needy. But Christian witness would be incomplete if the Church did not also have people like the Brazilian archbishop, Dom Helder Camara, who once said: "When I give food to the poor they call me a saint. When I ask why the poor have no food, they call me a communist." We must not be afraid to ask questions. For to give to the poor without asking *why* they are poor is to overlook an essential element of Christian charity, which is justice.

Justice demands equality in trading relationships. Yet many of our present trade structures uphold a system of inequalities which allows the rich to grow richer, while the poor develop slowly, if at all (cf. *Populorum Progressio,* par. 8). We all could—and should—have a part in righting the balance by refusing to go on enjoying the advantages of unequal trade structures. Paul VI posed the question that we should all be asking: Am I prepared "to pay more for imported goods, so that the foreign producer may make a fairer profit?" (cf. *Populorum Progressio,* par. 47). In other words, do I always look for the cheap bargain, even if I know it comes to me at someone else's expense? This is the sort of question that can help to create a greater awareness of at least some of the issues that lie behind the problem of world poverty. The gospel calls for justice as well as compassion for the poor, and this was the clear message of the 1971 Synod of Bishops: "Action on behalf of justice, and participation in the transformation of the world fully appear to us as a constitutive dimension of the preaching of the Gospel, or, in other words, of the Church's mission for the redemption of the human race and its liberation from every oppressive situation'' *(Justice in the World,* par. 6, Rome 1971).

Sadly, the contents of Pope Paul's encyclical and the document of the 1971 Synod have generally failed to penetrate the lives of those Christians who are able to enjoy the daily benefits of living in a highly industrialized society. They find the social dimension of the gospel quite disturbing and speak as if working for justice were an optional extra, failing to see it as an essential component of the Christian way of life. They are frightened to reflect seriously on these matters for fear that they might be unwilling or unable to meet the challenge of having to face a radical change of outlook.

The justice issue can bring home in a most uncomfortable way the choice which Jesus puts to his disciples: ''No one can be the slave of two masters: . . . you cannot be the slave of both God and money'' (Matt 6:24). It reminds us that following Jesus calls for a certain kind of lifestyle. The Christian has to witness by example as well as by words. People today are understandably tempted in the same way as Jesus' disciples were: ''This is a lonely place, and the time has slipped by, so send the people away, and they can go to the villages to buy themselves some food'' (Matt 14:15). The temptation to look elsewhere in the hope that the poor will solve their own problems is real. But Jesus still challenges us to share with them: ''How many loaves have you?'' (15:34).

I often receive letters from listeners to Radio 4's *Thought for the Day* who feel totally overwhelmed by the problems of injustice and poverty in the world. They frequently ask, ''What can I do? These problems are far too great for me to solve.'' I often feel the same sense of frustration, especially when I come face to face with the hungry in places like Brazil and Ethiopia. It is easy to give up for fear that one's efforts are futile.

The miracle of the loaves, as described by Matthew, can inspire us to overcome our hesitations and persevere in our efforts, no matter how insignificant these may appear to be. ''All we have with us is five loaves and two fish. . . . Now about five thousand men had eaten, to say nothing of women and children'' (Matt 14:18ff.). Faith teaches that Jesus Christ achieves great things through what at first sight appear to be insignificant efforts on the part of those who believe in him.

CHAPTER 10

An Ambitious Mother

Then the mother of Zebedee's sons . . . said to him, "Promise that these two sons of mine may sit one at your right hand and the other at your left in your kingdom." Jesus answered, "You do not know what you are asking. Can you drink from the cup that I am going to drink?" They replied, "We can."
—Matt 20:20-28

Jesus began his public ministry with the announcement that the kingdom of heaven was imminent (Matt 4:17). Matthew's Gospel is the story of how he set about establishing God's reign. His plan was an unpretentious as were the circumstances of his birth (see Matt 1:25). The kingdom would come so unobtrusively that its growth would be like that of a mustard seed (cf. Matt 13:31-32). But Matthew was anxious to show that the community founded by Jesus had a key role to play in the unfolding of this plan. They had been made responsible for the kingdom (Matt 16:18-19); they were partners in the new and everlasting covenant (Matt 26:28); they had been given authority to teach and to make new disciples (Matt 28:19-20).

Given the importance of their role, Matthew did not like to draw too much attention to the disciples' personal failings. An unconcealed ambition for power would not have enhanced the reputation of James and John within the community. So he added a new element to this incident, which had already been reported by Mark (10:38-40). By introducing a mother figure who seeks high office for her sons, Matthew hoped to cast the two

75

brothers in a more favorable light. For what could be more normal than a mother who pushes for the success of her children? Had not Solomon's mother, Bathsheba, done exactly that when she pleaded with King David on behalf of her son? (1 Kgs 1:11-40).

The other disciples "were indignant with the two brothers" (Matt 20:24)—probably because they, too, were ambitious for power and fame in this new kingdom proclaimed by Jesus. But unlike Luke (22:24), Matthew makes no mention of any power struggle among the disciples at this point, for according to his account they had already discussed the matter openly on a previous occasion. However, they had evidently failed to understand what Jesus had taught them: "The one who makes himself as little as this child is the greatest in the kingdom of Heaven" (Matt 18:4). So the misplaced ambition of James and John gave Jesus the opportunity to reiterate his teaching on the true nature of discipleship.

He did not denounce the apostles' ambition to succeed but instead clarified the meaning of success in terms of the new kingdom. They had to learn to think in a totally new way, to understand that what the world had come to spurn was valued most highly by God. The disciple was called to a life of service: "Anyone who wants to become great among you must be your servant, and anyone who wants to be first among you must be your slave" (Matt 20:27-28). Self-denial—rather than self-assertion—was the way to success in God's kingdom. "Anyone who does not take up his cross and follow in my footsteps is not worthy of me" (Matt 10:38).

So, into their squabble over rank, Jesus projects the ideal of service. They will succeed, he tells them, insofar as they model their lives on his: "The Son of Man came not to be served but to serve, and to give his life as a ransom for many" (Matt 20:28). A slave has no alternative but to put himself at the disposal of others; he cannot claim any right in order to protect his own interests. And that is the degree of service Jesus expects from his followers.

In making such a demand he stands on their head all the values and ambitions of the world. The disciple must learn to stifle the desire for worldly importance in order to surrender totally to God (cf. Matt 16:24-26). There is no alternative, for there is no shortcut to success—as Jesus realized in the wilderness when he rejected Satan's proposals for the instant success of his own mission (see Matt 4:1-11). The disciples also would have to face up to the same sorts of temptations and learn to resist them. Power politics and self-serving ambition have no place in the service of that kingdom which Jesus came to establish.

Matthew's community would have understood at once the significance of Jesus' question: "Can you drink the cup that I am going to drink?" (20-22). The cup was a symbol of fellowship and shared destiny. At meals, where the custom was to pass round a cup so that all could drink from it, those who did so expressed their willingness to stand together and to share whatever blessings or misfortunes life might bring. The psalmist spoke of the cup in terms of comfort and happiness: "The Lord is my cup . . . so my heart rejoices, my soul delights. . . . You will teach me the path of life, unbounded joy in your presence, at your right hand delight for ever" (Ps 16). In contrast, the prophet Isaiah spoke of it in terms of suffering and sorrow (Isa 51:17). When Jesus spoke of the cup he was referring to his own sufferings—as the fact that Matthew chose to place this story immediately after Jesus' prediction that he would die on the cross (Matt 20:17-19) makes abundantly clear. Success in the kingdom depends on the disciple's willingness to share, not just the fellowship of Jesus but also his suffering—the cross.

In the Book of Deuteronomy we read: "If a man guilty of a capital offense is to be put to death, and you hang him from a tree, his body must not remain on the tree overnight; you must bury him the same day, since anyone hanged is a curse of God" (Deut 21:22-23). Any form of public execution—including crucifixion—was a sign of shame and clear evidence that God had abandoned the individual concerned. That is why Peter protested so urgently at the very suggestion that Jesus might be put to death

on a cross: "Heaven preserve you Lord," he said, "this must not
happen to you" (Matt 16:22). But Jesus rebuked him, warning
him not to allow his human way of thinking to get in the way
of God's plan; that would be to play right into the hands of the
devil. "Get behind me Satan! You are an obstacle in my path,
because you are thinking not as God thinks but as human beings do" (16:23).

Isaiah had already predicted how things would turn out for
the Messiah (chs. 40–55), who was to make amends for the sins
of others by his suffering and death (Isa 53:1-12). Jesus realized
that he had to take on the role of this "suffering servant," and
that his own death would be a cause of scandal to onlookers: "He
had no form or charm to attract us, no beauty to win our hearts;
he was despised, the lowest of men, a man of sorrows, familiar
with suffering, one from whom, as it were, we averted our gaze,
despised, for whom we had no regard" (Isa 53:2-3).

There was no alternative. Only by suffering and dying for
the sake of others could Jesus successfully fulfill his mission and
break down all the barriers that existed between God and his
people. His death on the cross would demonstrate unquestion-
ably that no one was beyond the reach of God's love—not even
the common criminal who until then had been despised and rejected by the whole community.

In other words, Jesus' death extended the boundaries of the
kingdom. There was no such thing as an outsider, a nonstarter
where God's love was concerned (cf. Gal 3:13). As God's lowly
servant, Jesus invited all peoples to share in his fellowship (cf.
Isa 42:1-4).

But anyone invited to share in his fellowship was expected
to share in his destiny as well. The disciples had to learn to model
their lives not only on the words of Jesus but also on his example.
There was only one way to success in the new kingdom, through
self-denial and the way of the cross. There could be no instant
salvation.

Matthew's account of this incident with the sons of Zebedee points forward to his account of the Last Supper, when Jesus

invited all of those present to share in his cup: "Then he took a cup, and when he had given thanks he handed it to them saying, 'Drink from this, all of you, for this is my blood, the blood of the covenant, poured out for many for the forgiveness of sins'" (Matt 26:27-28).

Matthew wanted to place the disciples' call to service within a Eucharistic context. His community were by then familiar with the practice of sharing the common cup every time they gathered to celebrate the Eucharistic meal, and he was anxious to remind them of the profound spiritual and practical implications of their action. To share in the cup was to renew one's personal commitment to the new covenant of which it was a symbol—and which had been written "not on stone tablets, but on the tablets of human hearts" (2 Cor 3:3) and sealed by the shedding of Jesus' blood on the cross.

Jeremiah the prophet foretold that God would not allow sin and guilt to come between himself and his people forever (see Jer 31:31-34). Jesus, as the Christ, had proved the truth of this "by sacrificing himself" (Heb 9:26). Despite his feelings of anguish, sadness, and fear at the very thought of the cross, Jesus persevered with the mission God had entrusted to him: "My Father," he said, "if this cup cannot pass by, but I must drink it, your will be done!" (Matt 26:42). He was able to offer what the prophets Hosea and Amos had called for, a sacrifice completely rooted in faithful and loving service of God (cf. Hos 6:6 and Amos 5:21).

This gave the followers of Jesus the confidence to face God (cf. 2 Cor 3:4). No longer were they to regard themselves as outsiders or to remain content with being mere onlookers. The new covenant, effectively symbolized in their Eucharistic worship, called for direct involvement; it obliged them to participate fully in the life of Jesus. Their Eucharistic worship would help them to keep the true nature of their vocation—a life of self-giving service—firmly in focus. In particular, sharing the Eucharistic cup would enable them to embrace the cross in their own lives without fear of failure: "Anyone who loses his life for my sake will find it" (Matt 10:39).

Matthew's account of how Jesus handled the misguided ambitions of James and John should encourage as well as enlighten us. Day and night these two men shared the company of Jesus. They had every opportunity to observe his actions and listen to his words. Yet both, it seems, utterly failed to grasp what Jesus' life and message were really about. When they expressed their ambition for success they were obviously thinking—as Jesus' answer indicates—of the sort of power and prestige that success in purely human terms would bring (see Matt 20:25). What they must have wanted was some sort of reassurance that they had not wasted their lives in following him.

Surprisingly, Jesus did not admonish them for their failure to understand his message. He simply took the opportunity to correct their mistaken vision of the new kingdom. His reaction to their lack of insight and understanding should reassure us. We, too, need time to understand the full practical implications of accepting the gospel, and we should not be tempted to give up walking in his company because we do not yet understand, let alone reflect, Jesus' example of total self-giving.

It is important for us to remember that, although when the cross became a reality "all the disciples deserted him and ran away" (Matt 26:56), this did not prevent Jesus from seeking out their company again after his resurrection (see Matt 28:10). He was still prepared to entrust them with the continuation of his own God-given mission: "All authority in heaven and on earth has been given to me. Go, therefore, make disciples of all nations. . ." (Matt 28:18-19).

In other words, our lack of understanding and even our mistakes need not get in the way of God's trust in us, provided we are open to correction and are willing to learn. Jesus, Matthew reminds us, admonished Jerusalem not for its failure to understand but for its refusal to learn. It was not open to receive the wisdom of God: "How often have I longed to gather your children as a hen gathers her chicks under her wings, and you refused!" (Matt 23:37).

The call to live continually in the shadow of the cross is not an invitation to a life of doom and gloom. On the contrary, the cross, properly understood, spells freedom and hope. Only faith can help us to understand this paradox: "We are preaching a crucified Christ; to the Jews an obstacle they cannot get over, to the Gentiles foolishness, but to those who have been called, whether they are Jews or Gentiles, a Christ who is both the power and the wisdom of God. God's folly is wiser than human wisdom, and God's weakness is stronger than human strength" (1 Cor 1:23-25).

The early Christians did not find it easy to accept the cross as a symbol of their faith, since at the human level it stood only for failure. The full horror, and indeed the scandal, of what happened to Jesus was far too real for them to be comfortable with such a contradictory sign. But looking with the eyes of faith, they learned to regard the cross—God's folly—as the symbol of success. It taught them not to be frightened of the unexpected; it enabled them to face each day with confidence despite the uncertainties and even the open hostility they frequently experienced (cf. Acts 4:13-21; 8:1-3). It did not allow them to give way to despair but stood in their midst as a sign of hope.

The message of the cross has not changed. It is the sign of our assured success. The cross teaches us to overcome our fear of failure and to grow through the mistakes we inevitably make. Far from encouraging us to take refuge in a dream world where problems can be avoided, it enables us to face these problems, which might otherwise become a source of frustration and despair, as challenges within our control. It will not anaesthetize our pain, remove our sense of emptiness and loneliness, or allow us to suppress our feelings of grief and sadness. It will certainly not guarantee a life free of care. But it will oblige today's disciple to face up to the sort of problems he or she would naturally prefer to avoid.

The paradox of the cross still stands. When I look at the image of the cross which hangs on the wall of my room, not only does it remind me of the true nature of the Christian vocation, it also enables me to give an overall meaning and purpose to my life—in other words, to make sense of what could otherwise be described as a fairly chaotic day. It helps me not to feel trapped within my mistakes while teaching me the importance of continually examining the motives behind my own behavior. The cross is a sober reminder that Christianity is not a religion for philosophical onlookers. It is a call to daily communion with the Suffering Servant of Isaiah. And that requires a willingness to pay the same price as Jesus paid for his active involvement in the lives of others: "Can you drink from the cup that I am going to drink?" (Matt 20:22).

St. Paul, in his letter to the Philippians, quotes one of the oldest liturgical hymns, which describes how Jesus emptied himself and became a slave (see Phil 2:5-11). Jesus' total involvement in the human condition points the way for those who would follow him. "Nothing is to be done out of jealousy or vanity; instead, out of humility of mind everyone should give preference to others, everyone pursuing not selfish interests but those of others" (Phil 3:3-4). This, says St. Paul, is how the disciple will enter into the mind of Christ and discover the true meaning of the cross in his or her own life. His message is unambiguous: through the cross God identifies with us in our confusion and emptiness. He is not deterred by any human condition or experience but reaches out in particular to those who feel lost or marginal (Matt 18:10-14).

Awareness of what the cross means will not make self-denial for the sake of others any easier. It would be folly to imagine that we can live for others, saying no to our own perfectly legitimate desires, and at the same time avoid the inevitable pain involved. The ideal of service which Jesus sets before us requires that we surrender ourselves totally to God's loving care, relaxing that tight control over our affairs which most of us are anxious to maintain because it gives us a sense of security. To allow the needs of others to determine one's daily program means being available and ready to respond, whether it is personally convenient or not.

That becomes possible when we learn to root our need for security in God alone. Then we discover, in the shadow of the cross, that all our human values in terms of loss and gain have been totally reversed: "Anyone who wants to save his life will lose it; but anyone who loses his life for my sake will find it" (Matt 16:25). Success is to be judged in terms not of what we gain but of what we learn to give.

CHAPTER 11

A Surprise Invitation

Then he said to his servants, "The wedding is ready; but those who were invited proved to be unworthy. Go to the main crossroads and invite everyone you can find to come to the wedding." So these servants went out onto the roads and collected together everyone they could find, bad and good alike; and the wedding hall was filled with guests. When the king came in to look at the guests he noticed one man who was not wearing a wedding garment. . . .

—Matt 22:1-14

A notable feature in all four Gospels is Jesus' ability as a storyteller. But the stories he told were not just ordinary ones, they were parables. He had mastered the technique of taking an ordinary everyday experience and relating it in such a way that his listeners gained a new insight into life. The parable was an effective way of catching people's immediate attention and challenging their old ways of thinking. Its aim was to get people to act on the message it conveyed. The literary style of a parable could vary—when it was also allegorical each detail stood for a particular person or event that would have been known to those listening.

The parables in general are considered to be among the most authentic expressions of Jesus to be found in the Gospels. Even so, when we read them we do need to remember that half a century or more had passed between Jesus' telling of a story and Matthew's written version. In the meantime they had been passed on by word of mouth from one community to another. The original was sometimes modified or adapted in order to address more directly the changed circumstances and new problems these communities were having to face. The parable of the wedding feast is a case in point.

Jesus' original story was probably much shorter. Time and again he found himself being criticized, especially by the religious leaders, for the type of company he chose to keep—sinners and tax collectors were frequently found at his table, sharing his bread. The religious leaders were genuinely shocked; these were the outcasts, the despised, the nonconformists of their society. How could Jesus invite such people to share his table? No genuine "holy" person would want to associate with types like this even in private, let alone in public (cf. Matt 9:10-13).

Jesus realized that they simply did not understand the nature and extent of God's love and mercy (cf. Matt 11:25-27). He needed to tell them a story that would effectively convey his own insights into that love and at the same time justify his readiness to eat in the company of sinners. The fact was that the religious leaders had no grounds for complaint. They received an invitation to share his table and had rejected it, leaving room for those whom they regarded totally unworthy of sharing in God's love. To criticize his attitude and behavior toward sinners was in effect to suggest that God's love can somehow be limited.

Matthew expanded Jesus' original parable so as to help his own community understand some of the serious problems they were having to face. The Jewish leaders were openly hostile, continually questioning the disciples' authority to preach and to form new communities—especially when those included Gentiles (cf. Acts 4:1-4; 18:13). Matthew's aim was to provide them with an apologia for their own existence and their mission to the Gentiles. He turned Jesus' parable into an allegorical summary of the history of salvation. Every detail was significant. His message was clear: the people of Israel, through their own fault, no longer had an exclusive claim to God's love. God's embrace included Gentiles, the very people who had previously been considered beyond his reach.

The first servants were the prophets: their message had been rejected (v. 3). Then came the apostles: their message had also been rejected, and some of them had been put to death (vv. 4-7). The destruction of "their town" probably refers to the fall of Jerusalem, which was sacked by the Roman armies in A.D. 70. The servants sent "out onto the roads" (v. 10) were undoubtedly themselves and their mission to the Gentiles. Matthew continues his account into the future, right up to the moment of judgment when they would be called to give an account of their stewardship (vv. 11-13).

As Matthew uses it, the story is more than a polemic against the Jewish leaders; it also carries a warning for the members of his own community. They should not take their faith for granted. The "wedding garment" underlines their moral responsibility to live up to the expectations of their faith. What had happened to the people of Israel could also happen to them. They could—and it seems that some of them already had—become lukewarm in their commitment to Jesus Christ. The man without a wedding garment was silent; he had no excuse to offer. They too would have no excuse should they fail to respond wholeheartedly to God's call (v. 12).

The "wedding feast" had long been a symbol of the joy and happiness of the messianic age. Isaiah looked forward to the divine banquet to which all nations would be invited: "On this mountain, for all peoples, the Lord God is preparing a banquet of rich food, a banquet of fine wines. On this mountain he has destroyed the veil which is used to veil all peoples, the pall enveloping all nations: he has destroyed death for ever" (Isa 25:6-8). Matthew clearly believed that the coming of Jesus had inaugurated the messianic age: "My banquet is all prepared, my oxen and fattened cattle have been slaughtered, everything is ready. Come to the wedding" (22:5). The new community should reflect the spirit of that divine banquet. The invitation to share in the joy and happiness Jesus brought into the world was made to all, but from each it required a wholehearted personal response. The Christian was expected to live out his or her life in keeping with God's call.

It is not easy for us today to appreciate fully the significance behind the details of this parable. To begin with, we have very different marriage customs. In Matthew's day, guests were not normally told in advance exactly when a celebration would begin. Once the invitation had gone out they were expected to be ready to receive the summons to the banquet. To be preoccupied with one's own business or to arrive without the customary dress would have been taken as a sign of indifference or even contempt for the host. What Matthew was saying was that the established religious leaders had received the call but were unprepared to live in the messianic age established by Jesus. They refused to break bread with him and to share in his fellowship. This should serve as a warning for the new community, the young Church. Its members were just as vulnerable: they too could become preoccupied and fail to respond to the Lord's arrival at the unexpected hour: "You too must stand ready because the Son of Man is coming at an hour you do not expect" (Matt 24:44).

Once we have received the invitation to faith, the Lord expects to find us ready and dressed in our "wedding garment." And that garment is not one that we can buy "off the peg [rack]." It is woven around us as we reach out to the hungry, the thirsty, the stranger, the naked, the sick, and the imprisoned. Active concern for the poor and the needy is what proves our readiness to receive the Lord when he comes. Faith expressed in this way qualifies us for a place at his banquet:

> Come, you whom my Father has blessed, take as your heritage the kingdom prepared for you since the foundation of the world. For I was hungry and you gave me food, I was thirsty and you gave me drink, I was a stranger and you made me welcome, lacking clothes and you clothed me, sick and you visited me, in prison and you came to see me. . . . Insofar as you did this to one of the least of these brothers of mine, you did it to me (Matt 25:31-46).

We will be judged on the quality of our mercy. Faith calls for action on behalf of the poor, and human compassion is the "fruit" required from every disciple. This fruit the Pharisees and Sadducees had failed to produce (cf. Matt 3:7-10). Their uprightness alone would not qualify them for "entry into the kingdom of Heaven" (Matt 5:20). True discipleship calls for more than a public profession of faith (cf. Matt 10:32), prayer, prophecy, or even the working of miracles and the casting out of demons (cf. Matt 7:21-23).

The Letter of James, which was probably written some years before Matthew's Gospel, emphasizes that practical concern for those in need is an essential requirement of the Christian faith: "If one of the brothers or one of the sisters is in need of clothes and has not enough food to live on, and one of you says to them, 'I wish you well, keep yourself warm and eat plenty,' without giving them these bare necessities of life, then what good is that? In the same way faith: if good deeds do not go with it, it is quite dead" (Jas 2:15-17). Faith will bring a sense of messianic joy and happiness into our lives only insofar as we recognize our moral responsibility to help those in need.

To attempt to live a life of faith without genuine compassion for the poor stands in the same category as the man who entered the wedding feast without his wedding garment—and when confronted by Christ he will have no choice but to remain silent (v. 12), embarrassed by his or her failure to grasp the true significance of his words: "In truth I tell you, insofar as you neglected to do this to one of the least of these, you neglected to do it to me" (Matt 25:45). Our presence in the banqueting hall (our membership of the Church community) is not sufficient to guarantee us a place at the Lord's table (eternal life). Faith calls for a conscientious response involving the whole person—heart, mind, and body (cf. Matt 13:4-43). An unproductive servant cannot expect to find a place reserved at God's table (cf. Matt 21:33-43). Action on behalf of the needy is an indispensable part of our response to God's call.

The first generation of Christians believed that Jesus' return in glory was imminent—which in some ways made their response to faith that much easier. Matthew's community, on the other hand, had more than fifty years' experience of Christian life to reflect on. Their awareness and expectations had matured in the light of this experience. They knew how easy it was to be distracted or to become preoccupied with other matters. Matthew wanted to encourage them to persevere in their initial response to God's call. He was anxious to challenge any complacency that might have crept into their way of thinking or behaving. They needed to be on their guard, to be ready to receive the Lord whenever he came: "So stay awake, because you do not know either the day or the hour" (Matt 25:13). The Lord's coming was not to be as soon as they had expected: "The bridegroom was late" (Matt 25:5). But this was no excuse for lack of diligence. The Lord might be going to come unexpectedly, but come he would. So the fatigue that comes from simply waiting around must not be allowed to get in the way of their response (cf. Matt 25:1-13).

All this is true for us too. We can so easily give in to fatigue, to discouragement at the Lord's apparent delay in making his presence really felt in our lives. We can so easily become preoccupied with matters of secondary importance. Nor is our moral weakness the only thing that gets in the way of our response to God: sometimes we take on unconsciously the role of those in the parable who were too busy to respond immediately: "One went off to his farm, another to his business" (v. 6). Work, the pursuit of wealth, and even active involvement in the affairs of others must not be allowed to distract our attention from the main purpose of our lives, which is to be found in Jesus Christ. Faith requires that we lay ourselves open to being "molded to the pattern" of God's Son (cf. Rom 8:29-30).

To end on a personal note, I get great encouragement from this particular parable. It underlines for me the tremendous patience of God, who continually reaches out in search of human company. God has never been put off by our failure to respond but time and again renews his offer of a place at his banquet. Today, that same patient God is inviting us to be among his table companions.

CHAPTER 12

Faith and Political Action

But Jesus was aware of their malice and replied, "You hypo-crites! Why are you putting me to the test? Show me the money you pay tax with." They handed him a denarius, and he said, "Whose portrait is this? Whose title?" They replied, "Caesar's." Then he said to them, "Very well, pay Caesar what belongs to Caesar—and God what belongs to God."
—Matt 22:15-22

This passage is frequently quoted to justify the argument that the Church should not be involved in any form of political debate or action. Religion, its supporters say, is a private matter involving the individual's personal response to God; it has nothing to do with the day-to-day running of a country, which is purely a secular matter. But is that really what Jesus meant when he said: "Pay to Caesar what belongs to Caesar—and to God what belongs to God"? Was Matthew telling his community that the best way to relate to their civil authorities was to keep out of politics?

Matthew leaves us in no doubt that the Pharisees' question was insincere. Their prime purpose in asking it was to set a trap for Jesus (cf. 22:15). They knew that if he were to acknowledge Rome's right to collect tax he would lose credibility with the people, most of whom were utterly opposed to the taxation laws on religious grounds. On the other hand, if he were publicly to oppose the payment of tax he would find himself in open conflict with the Roman authorities. Either way, they hoped, the result would be the same: his influence would be curbed. Jesus, however, was aware of their intentions (v. 18). Refusing to be drawn, he neatly sidestepped their question by turning the attention back on to them: "Show me the money you pay tax with" (v. 19).

By asking them to produce the coin that was used for paying tax, Jesus exposed their lack of sincerity. They had already compromised themselves by the fact that they possessed—and presumably made use of—Roman money. So, if they were prepared to benefit from the Roman system when it was in their interest, why should they object to paying tax—to paying Caesar "what belongs to Caesar"? (v. 21).

Having said that, although Matthew was clearly more interested in exposing the shallowness of Jesus' critics than in providing successive generations of Christians with the governing principle for good Church-State relationships, he was certainly not teaching that Christians should consider their political life as something entirely separate from their faith. On the contrary, he stresses that the loyalty we owe to God should never be overlooked (vv. 22-21)—and that can have profound political implications.

St. Paul had already touched on the problem of relationships with the State in some of his letters, which were written years before Matthew compiled his Gospel. Believing that Christians were subject to the civil law like everyone else (cf. Rom 13:1-7)—that they should even pray for those in civil authority (cf. 1 Tim 2:1)—he saw no reason for conflict between faith and political activity. His attitude was influenced by his belief in Jesus' imminent return: anxious that Christians should not be unnecessarily provocative, he encouraged them to live "peaceful and quiet lives" (cf. 1 Thess 5:1-11) as they waited for the Lord to come in glory (1 Tim 2:2). Similar ideas are to be found in the First Letter of Peter (2:13-17). But when it came to unavoidable conflict with the civil authorities, both Paul and Peter insisted that "obedience to God comes before obedience to men" (Acts 5:30).

Since both are concerned with how we relate to one another and organize our lives in community, faith and politics cannot be separated. If politics concerns the whole person, so too does the gospel. There must be an interplay between them, a point of overlap where religious beliefs find their rightful expression in political judgments and activities. Some present-day anxieties concerning the interaction of faith and politics are no doubt based on the Church's record in the past. And certainly many examples can be found of churchmen who misused political power in the furtherance of their own ambitions. But Christians today should not use the mistakes of the past as an excuse for not taking their own responsibility seriously. We are called to give unambiguous witness to gospel values in every aspect of our lives—including our political judgments. Problems relating to unemployment, homelessness, health care, education, defense, and industrial strife should indeed concern us. They affect people and the way they relate to one another and in that sense touch the very heart of the gospel. We should examine these controversial issues in the light of the gospel and should not be frightened to speak out accordingly.

The Second Vatican Council recognized this as our legitimate role in society. Its *Pastoral Constitution on the Church in the Modern World* claims that our aim should be to make political life more truly human. This we will achieve by fostering justice and kindliness at every level and by promoting the common good above individual selfish interests. The political community and civil authority exist solely for the common good; the Church should continually remind society of this.

> It is for them [Christians] to give an example by their sense of responsibility and their service of the common good. . . . With integrity and wisdom they must take action against any form of injustice and tyranny, against arbitrary domination by an individual or a political party, and any intolerance. They should dedicate themselves to the service of all, with sincerity and fairness, indeed with the charity and fortitude demanded by political life (*Gaudium et Spes*, par. 75, in *Proclaiming Justice and Peace*, CAFOD/Collins).

Pope John XXIII also encouraged Christians to take an active part in public life. He believed it was the Church's duty to concern itself with the full spiritual and material growth of the human person. To do this effectively and to "imbue civilization with right ideals and Christian principles," it would have to become involved in the economic, social, cultural, and political debate. John warned, though, against self-seeking on the part of the Church, whose ambition must always be to serve; it must forgo the desire for human power and influence (cf. his encyclical letter *Pacem in Terris* on establishing universal peace). Both the motivation and the example for our involvement in human affairs are provided by Jesus: "The Son of Man came not to be served but to serve, and to give his life as a ransom for many" (Matt 20:28).

A friend, who for many years worked as a missionary priest in the Philippines, told me that when he first went there he was sent to an area where there was serious tension between the landowners and the peasant farmers. Faced with this conflict, he believed that the best thing he could do was to act as a reconciler. For several years he tried to lessen the tensions and to keep some sort of peace in the local community. One day a poor man came to him, complaining that a landowner had thrown him off his farm. He listened patiently as the man explained the problem. Then, "I'll pray for you, that's all I can do," he said. The poor farmer just stared at the priest in silence. That empty look was sufficient to convince my friend that he could no longer remain neutral; in this situation he had to take sides.

His experience illustrates what has happened to the Church in general over the past twenty years. At one time, most Christians believed that in situations of conflict and social unrest they should not take sides—to do so would be to jeopardize the prime role of the Church in society, which was to work for reconciliation. But in our desire to lessen tensions and promote reconciliation, we frequently overlooked the injustices that had given rise to the conflicts and social unrest. Today the approach of the Church in general is different. What is happening in South Africa, in the Philippines, in Brazil, and in many other parts of the world is a good illustration of this.

Pope Paul VI attributed this change of attitude within the Church to the fact that we have become more deeply aware of what it means to say that the human person is made "in the image and likeness of God" (Gen 1:27). We now understand that all persons are essentially equal and should be given the opportunity to develop their potential to the full. The Church consequently believes that the promotion of human rights is required by the gospel and is an essential part of her own ministry, both to the community and to individuals (cf. Paul VI, apostolic letter *Evangelii Nuntiandi*, on evangelization in the modern world).

In practical terms, this new awareness means that Christians who find themselves caught up in conflict have no alternative but to take sides. In clear instances of oppression and injustice, it would be inconceivable for Christians not to be on the side of the victim—to remain neutral would be seriously to damage the credibility of the gospel message. This does not mean that we have abandoned our role as reconcilers. Quite the opposite, but we have come to realize, more fully perhaps than before, that reconciliation and peace will not be genuine or lasting unless they are founded upon justice.

The Brazilian bishop, Don Helder Camara, tells how he was once invited to celebrate Mass at the ranch of a wealthy landowner. He arrived to find that hundreds of workers were also present. "How will I preach?" he asked himself. He knew that if he told them to do their duty conscientiously and to obey their employer, he would be seen in the eyes of the landowner at least, as a "holy" bishop. If, on the other hand, he had the audacity to suggest that workers also had rights which the landowner should respect, he would probably be labeled "progressive" or "procommunist."

His story is not an isolated one. It illustrates the kind of dilemma that frequently inhibits Christians from taking sides or becoming openly involved in the public debate on issues of social concern. Am I prepared to speak out in defense of someone else's rights, even at the risk of being labeled? Or do I allow the fear that I will be accused of being one-sided to force me into silence, even if that means ignoring my fundamental beliefs? The problem for the Christian is that the beliefs and values he or she is called to uphold are not always generally acceptable, especially in an affluent society. The temptation to be halfhearted or luke-warm in one's witness is very real. Few people enjoy the thought of receiving a public rebuke; no one likes to lose friends and poten-tial allies. We are tempted to search for compromises, and when we find them our witness to the values of the gospel tends to be ambiguous or ineffective.

Matthew tells the story of the rich young man who came to Jesus in search of eternal life (see Matt 19:16-22). He had led a good life and had kept all the commandments, but he felt there was still something lacking. Jesus took an immediate liking to this young man (cf. Mark 10:21) but did not allow his feelings to determine his response: he was direct in his criticism, telling the young man that he was too attached to his wealth. This di-rect approach was too much for the young man to take; he walked away and Jesus lost a friend.

Most Christians find it extremely difficult to follow Jesus' example in this respect, and I believe that is one reason why we are frequently tempted to separate our beliefs from our politics. By not taking sides, or by trying to avoid direct public involve-ment in contentious social and moral issues, we find it much easier to keep our reputation and our friends. But the cost of such a compromise could indeed be great. As Jesus himself asked: "What, then, will anyone gain by winning the whole world and forfeiting his life?" (Matt 16:26). The only way the Christian can secure his or her life is by learning "to renounce himself and take up his cross" (Matt 16:24-25). In practice this may well mean having, at times, to let go of both reputation and friends.

CHAPTER 13

Mission Made Possible

Meanwhile the eleven disciples set out for Galilee, to the mountain where Jesus had arranged to meet them. When they saw him they fell down before him, though some hesitated. Jesus came up and spoke to them. He said, "All authority in heaven and on earth has been given to me. Go, therefore, make disciples of all nations; baptize them in the name of the Father and of the Son and of the Holy Spirit, and teach them to observe all the commands I gave you. And look, I am with you always; yes, to the end of time."

—Matt 28:16-20

Belief in the resurrection of Jesus permeates Matthew's Gospel. Matthew fully believed that Jesus had risen from the dead, and he was anxious to share this belief and all it implied with his own community. But he was interested in the resurrection as an event of faith rather than as an event in history, and this naturally influenced his presentation of the facts. He had no intention of providing a detailed account of what happened—he even chose to omit some details related by St. Paul and the other gospel writers (cf. 1 Cor 15:3-8; John 21:9-14). Yet brief as his account may be, it nevertheless alludes to the sort of phenomena that had come to be associated with the direct intervention of God: "And suddenly there was a violent earthquake, for an angel of the Lord, descending from heaven, came and rolled away the stone and sat on it. His face was like lightning, his robe white as snow" (Matt 28:2-3). The Book of Exodus uses similar imagery to describe the meeting between God and Moses on Mount

Sinai (19:16-25). And the angel who showed the two women into the empty tomb (Matt 28:1-7) reminds us of Daniel's apparition on the bank of the river Tigris (Dan 10:4-7).

Matthew was clearly using these images to establish his belief that Jesus' resurrection was the result of God's direct intervention, to be understood as an essential part of God's plan for human salvation. He could confidently dismiss the deceitful claim of the chief priests and elders that it was a hoax (cf. Matt 28:11-15).

The empty tomb was simply a starting point for a whole new level of encounter with God: ''Filled with awe and great joy the women came quickly away from the tomb and ran to tell his disciples'' (Matt 28:8). Matthew, unlike Luke (24:9-12), saw no need for the others to come and inspect the tomb. The testimony of the women was enough to make them respond to Jesus' request: ''The eleven disciples set out for Galilee, to the mountain where Jesus had arranged to meet them'' (v. 16). Only faith would enable them to recognize as their risen Lord the Jesus who had been crucified (cf. Matt 28:5). ''When they saw him they fell down before him, though some hesitated'' (v. 17). Matthew was no doubt hoping to help the hesitaters in his community, those who were finding it difficult to believe in the resurrection because of the lack of firsthand evidence. He emphasizes here that faith requires a readiness to accept the word of another as a first step toward a personal encounter with the risen Lord.

Since there was no distinction between soul and body in Hebrew thought, to talk about resurrection was necessarily to imply some sort of physical resuscitation. The First Book of Kings tells how a widow's son was raised to life as a result of Elijah's prayers (1 Kgs 17:17-24), and a similar story is told in connection with Elisha (2 Kgs 4:18-37). In neither case is it suggested that the boy was restored to anything other than our present mode of life, still subject to decay.

It is the same with Matthew: when he tells how Jesus raised to life the daughter of a synagogue official (Matt 9:18-26), he too implies that she returned to life as we know it. The Sadducees, a strict religious sect, opposed the Pharisees on the question of the resurrection of the dead. They did not believe in it because they could find no evidence in their written tradition to support such a belief (cf. Matt 22:23). The Pharisees kept a more open mind, believing that somehow good upright people would be brought back to life.

In general, the Old Testament writings refer only vaguely to the idea of an afterlife. In the book of Isaiah, for example, we find the assertion: "Your dead will come back to life, your corpses will rise again" (Isa 26:19). The book of Maccabees, however, is quite explicit. As they were being tortured to death for their refusal to act against their beliefs, seven brothers challenged their executioner: "Cruel brute, you may discharge us from this present life, but the king of the world will raise us up, since we die for his laws, to live again for ever" (2 Macc 7:9). Slightly earlier, the Book of Daniel had spoken of "those who are sleeping in the land of dust," many of whom would "awaken, some to everlasting life, some to shame and everlasting disgrace" (Dan 12:2). It is clear that, at least among some Jews, a belief was beginning to develop in the power of the Creator to restore life. Jesus' resurrection brings a radically new dimension to this belief.

The risen Jesus was not a phantom. He was evidently recognizable as the person who had been crucified and was real enough to be touched: "And the women came up to him, and clasping his feet, they did him homage" (Matt 28:9). But he was more than a resuscitated corpse; there was a distinct difference between his resurrection and that of his friend Lazarus (see John 11:1-44). For although Jesus foretold his death and resurrection (cf. Matt 16:21; 17:9, 23), the disciples failed to understand its significance. Only experience would teach them the true meaning of what happened on the cross: that through his death God had conferred on Jesus a radically new form of life—a life that was neither subject to decay nor restricted by the limitations of time and space: "Go, therefore, make disciples of all nations. . . . I am with you always; yes, to the end of time" (Matt 28:19-20).

In other words, the death and resurrection of Jesus broke

down the barriers that sin had erected between God and humanity (cf. 1 Cor 15:3-5). This is the gospel—the good news that the disciples were sent to share with all men and women everywhere. God had found a permanent home in people's hearts. Through baptism they were called to share in this new life and to enjoy the fruits of Jesus' resurrection: "If the spirit of him who raised Jesus from the dead has made his home in you, then he who raised Christ Jesus from the dead will give life to your own mortal bodies through his spirit living in you" (Rom 8:11).

Belief in the resurrection gave a radically new perspective to the disciples' life of faith, bringing a sense of eternal life into their world of time. It taught them to revalue the whole purpose of life: "If Christ has not been raised, then our preaching is without substance and so is your faith. . . . If our hope in Christ had been for this life only, we are of all people the most pitiable" (1 Cor 15:14, 19). They too were called to experience resurrection: the power of God which was at work within Jesus would also be at work within them: "God raised up the Lord and he will raise us up too by his power" (1 Cor 6:15). This was a message which no doubt brought a real sense of "awe and great joy" into Matthew's community (Matt 28:8).

The experience of the resurrection completely transformed the lives of Jesus' disciples. It gave them a whole new outlook which enabled them to grow through the terrible trauma of the cross. Every one of them had been overcome by fear; they had deserted him and run away (see Matt 16:56). They had taken refuge behind closed doors, ashamed even to show their faces for fear that they might be recognized (cf. John 20:19).

But having encountered the risen Jesus, they felt compelled to give public witness to their new-found faith (cf. Acts 10:41-42). It was an experience that transformed a group of frightened fugitives into a company of fearless missionaries (Rom 1:3-5). Their example, more than their words, gave credence to their claim that Jesus had truly risen from the dead (cf. Acts 4:1-4).

Matthew's description of the first encounter between the risen Jesus and the disciples as a group reads like a summary of his

Gospel (cf. Matt 28:16-20). Jesus calls them together (cf. 4:18-22); he instructs them (cf. 5:1–7:29); he commissions them to make new disciples (cf. Matt 10:5-42); and he assures them of his supportive presence (cf. 14:22-23). Christian faith, in other words, is essentially missionary; it is a gift which should be shared with others. Just as Jesus' blood was "poured out for many" (Matt 26:28), so the Christian has to learn to live out his or her life for the sake of others (cf. Matt 20:27-28). It is in learning to let go of his or her narrow self-interests that the Christian begins to experience here and now that new life which the death and resurrection of Jesus brought into the world: "Anyone who wants to save his life will lose it; but anyone who loses his life for my sake will find it" (Matt 16:24-26).

Jesus' authority is a notable feature of his ministry throughout Matthew's Gospel: "His teaching made a deep impression on the people because he taught them with authority" (Matt 7:28-29). He used the same authority to forgive sins and to cure the sick: "But to prove to you that the Son of Man has authority on earth to forgive sins"—then he said to the paralytic—"Get up, pick up your bed and go off home" (Matt 9:6). Now Matthew has him make use of this same authority to establish the terms of the disciples' new mission which, contrary to his previous instructions (see Matt 10:5), was to include "all nations." At last the meaning of the parables of the wicked tenants (see Matt 21:33-46) and of the wedding feast (see Matt 22:1-14) was clear; the Gentiles were not to be excluded from the new community.

This was not an easy message for the disciples to absorb into their daily lives. The Acts of the Apostles does not disguise the fact that the baptism of the first Gentile quickly sparked off a controversy (see Acts 10:44-48ff.) which culminated in a public showdown between Peter and Paul (cf. Gal 2:11-14). In the end Paul established his right to preach the "Gospel for the uncircumcised" (Gal 2:7). By the time Matthew came to write his Gospel, he could confidently state that this was a message "for all nations."

That early controversy within the Christian community brings home to us that the gospel is essentially a mystery that unfolds through our attempts to live it. God's "ways" are not always immediately plain to us; he is frequently unpredictable: "You are thinking, not as God thinks but as human beings do" (Matt 16:23). When faced with the mystery of God in our lives we should never lose that sense of awe and wonder that keeps faith alive and joyful. As Paul once exclaimed: "How rich and deep are the wisdom and knowledge of God! We cannot reach to the root of his decisions or his ways. Who has ever known the mind of the Lord? Who has ever been his adviser?" (Rom 11:33-35).

Matthew is aware that Christians could easily fall into the same trap as the religious leaders who opposed Jesus (cf. Matt 16:1-12). To counteract that risk, he invites us to take a child as the pattern for our faith: "The one who makes himself as little as this little child is the greatest in the kingdom of Heaven" (Matt 18:4). Most children live in a world of awe and wonder, and it was precisely this mixture of "awe and great joy" which the two women experienced at finding the empty tomb—a discovery that led them to a direct encounter with the risen Jesus (28:8-10). Our faith will be vibrant only as long as we preserve the sense of awe and wonder it should bring to life.

In baptism the Christian is called to share in the mission which the risen Jesus gave to his disciples, called to "understand that God has no favorites, but that anybody of any nationality who fears him and does what is right is acceptable to him" (Acts 10:34-35). If this influences our lives as it should, it will be reflected in our attitudes and our overall outlook on things. It will help us to get rid of all traces of nationalism and to withstand the temptation to accept the present divided state of our world as inevitable. The Third Eucharistic Prayer of the Roman Missal asks the Lord "to advance the peace and salvation of all the world." The challenge for today's Christians is to believe that this goal is attainable and to work with God in achieving it. Faith in the resurrection will be their starting point and the point to which they constantly return. For in this perspective they will discover the unique value of each individual person irrespective of sex, age, country of origin, color, or social position.

And once they have taken hold of that, they will begin to realize their Christian calling: to witness that human life is a sacred gift that should always be protected and cherished.

Suggestions for Further Reading

Among the many interesting New Testament commentaries, I found the following books particularly helpful in coming to a better understanding of St. Matthew's Gospel:

The New Jerusalem Bible. Darton, Longman & Todd. Barclay, William. The Gospel of Matthew, Volumes 1 and 2. The Saint Andrew Press.

Boucher, Madeleine. The Parables. Veritas Publications.

Freyne, Sean. The World of the New Testament. Veritas Publications.

Harrington, Daniel J., S.J. Interpreting the New Testament. Veritas Publications.

Hendrickx, Herman. The Sermon on the Mount. Geoffrey Chapman.

_____. Passion Narratives. Geoffrey Chapman.

Lambrecht, Jan, S.J. The Sermon on the Mount. Michael Glazier.

Leon-Dufour, Xavier. Dictionary of Biblical Theology. Geoffrey Chapman.

McKenzie, John L., S.J. Dictionary of the Bible. Geoffrey Chapman.

Meier, John P. Matthew. Veritas Publications.

Nickle, Keith F. The Synoptic Gospels. S.C.M. Press.

Schweizer, Edward. The Good News According to Matthew. S.P.C.K.

Also Available from The Liturgical Press

Binz, Stephen. *The Passion and Resurrection Narratives of Jesus: A Commentary.*

Brown, Raymond E., S.S. *An Adult Christ at Christmas: Essays on the Three Biblical Christmas Stories—Matthew 2 and Luke 2.*

———. *A Coming Christ in Advent: Essays on the Gospel Narratives Preparing for the Birth of Jesus—Matthew 1 and Luke 1.*

———. *A Crucified Christ in Holy Week: Essays on the Four Gospel Passion Narratives.*

Ellis, Peter F. *Matthew: His Mind and His Message.*

Flanagan, Neal, O.S.M. *Mark, Matthew and Luke.*

Harrington, Daniel J., S.J. *The Gospel According to Matthew* (vol. 1: Collegeville Bible Commentary: New Testament series).